Effective Communication in Real Estate Management

Lyle Yorks

Associate Professor of Management
Eastern Connecticut State College
and
Senior Vice President
Drake-Beam and Associates
New York, New York

NATIONAL ASSOCIATION OF REALTORS®
Developed in cooperation with its affiliate, the
REALTORS NATIONAL MARKETING INSTITUTE®
of the NATIONAL ASSOCIATION OF REALTORS®
Chicago, Illinois

International Standard Book Number:
0-913652-21-0
Library of Congress Catalog Card Number:
79-67426
Marketing Institute Catalog Number: 135

Printed in the United States of America
First Printing, 1979, 10,000 copies

Interviewing model adapted from *Interviewing
for Managers*, by John D. Drake. New York:
AMACOM, copyright 1972. Used by
permission.

Certain materials in Chapter 2 adapted from
copyright material from Drake-Beam
Associates, New York. Used by permission.

"The Managerial Grid" by Robert R. Blake
and Jane S. Mouton, from *The New
Managerial Grid* (Houston: Gulf Publishing
Company) Copyright 1964; all rights reserved.

To Lyle, Tracy and Russell

About the Author

Lyle Yorks is an Associate Professor of Management Science at Eastern Connecticut State College and is a Senior Vice President with Drake-Beam & Associates in New York City. He consults with a wide variety of corporations on improving managerial communications, human resource utilization and related management development problems. Mr. Yorks has conducted management training programs throughout the United States, Canada, Europe and Latin America. Before joining Drake-Beam in 1972, he was an internal consultant for the Travelers Insurance companies in Hartford, Connecticut.

Mr. Yorks is the author of several management articles, and his book, *A Radical Approach to Job Enrichment* (AMACOM, 1976) was a selection of the Macmillan Executive Program Book Club. One of his articles, "A Time for Every Purpose" is included in *real estate today,®* *Ten Years of the Best.* (RNMI, 1978).

Contents

Acknowledgements

Many REALTORS® from around the United States assisted me in researching this book. I am most grateful for their cooperation in providing me access to their firms. I regret it is impossible to recognize each of their contributions since without their help there would be no book.

I would like to especially thank the following members of the REALTORS NATIONAL MARKETING INSTITUTE'S® Book Committee for spending time with me. Their insights and comments were most helpful.

James F. Bell, Jr., CCIM
Atlanta, GA

Howard C. Bissell, CCIM
Charlotte, NC

Lydia Franz, CRB
Barrington, IL

John W. Lane, Jr., CRB
Chicago, IL

Bernard J. MacElhenny, Jr., CRB
Santa Barbara, CA

Phillip M. Sleet, Jr., CRB, CRS
Alexandria, LA

Edward D. Surovell
Ann Arbor, MI

Judith P. Tibbetts, CRB
Darien, CT

Charles A. Trowbridge, CCIM
Denver, CO

I am most appreciative of the continuing interest and encouragement which has been provided by Peg Keilholz, my editor.

Special thanks must go to my wife, Joanne, whose contribution went significantly beyond that of tolerating the time the research and writing took away from my family. A newspaper journalist herself, she assisted in both the research and final editing of the manuscript. Her insightful comments were invaluable.

Preface

John Martin, a successful residential sales associate in a mid-western real estate firm has a lead on a good commercial property. Although his firm has a respected commercial department, he gives the lead to Will, a friend from another firm.

Allison Griffin has the highest production rate in her firm. Miffed because she was not named office manager, she seizes on every opportunity to criticize her broker.

A call from a prospect is taken by Mary Peters who has been with the firm two and a half weeks. Mary fumbles the call and the prospect decides to look elsewhere.

What these situations share in common is that each involves a communication problem. And they are not unique. They are representative of the kinds of problems which confront virtually any real estate broker or sales manager.

Communication is the cutting edge of effective management. It is the most pervasive aspect of organizational life, and the most elusive. Good communication must be developed. When effort is not put into communication, confusion and misunderstanding is the predictable result.

As a broker's firm grows in size, the communication problem becomes central to continued success. Suddenly the salesperson is a manager who, through persuasion and interpersonal influence, must elicit cooperation from his people.

The purpose of this book is to help real estate brokers and managers develop interpersonal communication skills useful in managing their sales and clerical support staff more effectively.[1] Most chapters are organized around a specific kind of communication setting such as managing conflict, giving criticism, staff selection, and motivation. Particular emphasis is placed on models and step-by-step approaches for handling these situations. Rather than attempt to give cookbook solutions which are limited in application, the intent is to provide the reader with process skills which will help the REALTOR® resolve a range of communication problems. Practical methods—not theory—for effective management of these activities are provided.

Using these methods requires skill. Where appropriate, exercises specifically designed to provide practice in the methods and techniques discussed in a chapter are provided. These exercises will assist the interested reader in skill development. Skill consists of more than memorizing technique; one must become sufficiently comfortable with the technique so that it blends with one's own aptitude and style.

The key to developing this kind of skill is practice. Initially, application of the methods may feel awkward. This is true when developing any new skill, whether it's serving a tennis ball, public speaking or selling. Gradually, however, awkwardness gives way to familiarity and application becomes almost automatic.

To facilitate the skill development process, the book has been written in a "building block" fashion. Many of the methods presented in a given chapter are built on the techniques and skills developed in preceding ones.

The methods and techniques presented in this book have demonstrated their effectiveness in a multitude of commercial and business management situations. Sales managers in a number of successful corporations have improved their organization's perfor-

---

[1]For simplicity's sake, the term broker includes all managers. Similarly, although the most frequent reference is to sales associates, the methods are applicable for communicating with non-sales personnel as well.

mance through these approaches. However, the material presented here has been adapted, following concentrated research, to the particular communication problems of REALTORS®.

There are no magic answers. No one can offer a formula which guarantees successful resolution of all the interpersonal communication problems which confront today's real estate executive. However, it is possible to develop skills which improve the batting average; skills which can help the REALTOR® avoid the more serious communication errors and build a stronger organization. It is toward this practical result that this book is directed.

Part I

The Art of Getting Through to Others

The success of any sales manager depends on the ability to communicate effectively. Whatever ideas, suggestions or expertise the broker may have is of little value if he or she cannot convey them to others.

As a successful broker expands his firm, his communication problems become more complex. The close, intimate feeling of the small office gives way to the diversity of the enlarged firm. People in different offices begin pulling in opposite directions. Under these circumstances, the broker's ability to communicate effectively becomes a critical determinant of whether the firm will continue to grow.

This book rests on the premise that managerial communication skills can be learned. Part I presents several core communication and problem-solving skills which are applicable in a wide range of real estate sales office situations. Each chapter in Part I builds on the material which has preceded it. Taken in their entirety chapters 1 through 4 provide skills germane to effective real estate office management.

Chapter 1
Interpersonal Communication: The Key to Managing Others

Why should the real estate broker or sales manager be concerned about developing his communication skills? The answer is straightforward: effective communication contributes to a more cost effective firm.

Operating in an industry experiencing rapid change in its competitive structure, today's broker must select, develop and retain the best people available to the firm. Whether the sales associates are independent contractors or employees, effective communication is important to good performance. Good communication skills are particularly important for the broker whose office is staffed with independent contractors since influence and persuasion, and not direction and control, are the means of eliciting cooperation and high performance.

It would be a mistake, of course, to limit our discussion solely to the sales associate. Communication skills are equally necessary when dealing with the clerical and administrative support staff. As one successful REALTOR® put it, "a firm which doesn't have the clerical support necessary to follow through on the sales effort is going to suffer the same as if the sales force was pulling in opposite directions."

Dissension or confusion resulting from poor communication can consume valuable staff time as sales associates and other key personnel divert energy away from their principal business activities. When a potential buyer or seller decides to look elsewhere for service because their call was handled poorly by an untrained or unprofessional sales associate, a part of the advertising budget has been wasted. And if a top salesperson leaves because he or she feels unappreciated, or resentful of certain office procedures (or any similar reason), replacing the lost production can be a difficult and expensive process. At a time when most brokers are experiencing rising desk costs, sound managerial communication skills are at the heart of an efficient office.

Simply put, a REALTOR® with nine salespeople and $16 million in sales is enjoying a larger return on his investment of time and money than a competitor in the same market with 35 salespeople and $21 million in sales. Inevitably, close observation reveals the former to be doing a more systematic job of managing and *communicating* with his people.

Most successful real estate executives accept a basic management fact: in building an organization they have to work almost entirely within the framework of other peoples' strengths and weaknesses. Such managers strive to identify, develop and utilize the talents of their people to the fullest possible extent.

Working within the framework of other people's strengths and weaknesses requires astute interpersonal skills. In a classic article on management, Robert Katz identified human skill (interpersonal skill) as a major component of effective administration.[1] Few serious thinkers on the subject have chosen to disagree with him. More importantly, experience bears out his argument. Consider the following situation:

Jack Winter
New Sales Director

Jack Winter has recently been appointed sales director over seven branch offices. His responsibilities include helping office managers develop their REALTOR-ASSOCIATE® staffs, centralizing the company's promotion efforts and establishing expense controls over the seven offices. Jack's company is going through a period of rapid expansion; several new branch offices were opened during the past couple of years. Jack, himself, has been with the company for five years.

During his first two and half years, he quickly established himself as an outstanding sales producer. Next, Jack assumed managerial responsibility for a new branch office and once more met with rapid success. The principal partners established the position of sales director to take advantage of Jack's considerable talent in establishing control over their expanding enterprise and to keep Jack challenged and happy with the company.

One of Jack's first procedural initiatives centered around purchasing office supplies, equipment and furniture. Traditionally, branch managers had enjoyed considerable latitude in purchasing items of this nature. Two months ago, Jack sent a memo to all the branch managers directing them to submit requisitions to him for supplies totaling more than twenty dollars. This would help the company retain control over expenditures and save money through centralized buying. In his memo, Jack asked the branch managers for their cooperation.

Two months later nothing had happened. No requisitions had appeared on Jack's desk for approval. In thinking about this, it seemed to Jack that there were three possible explanations. The branch managers might simply be ignoring his instructions. Or they were not making any more purchases over twenty dollars because such purchases were no longer required—a situation Jack felt was unlikely. Or these managers were manipulating their purchases to avoid making any over twenty dollars. If this last were the case, the managers were abiding by the letter if not the spirit of his instructions.

The more Jack thought about the situation, the more uneasy he became. Should he follow his instincts and either investigate or confront the managers? Or should he ask the principal partners to help him obtain more cooperation from the branch managers? Either course of action would place him in a position he had hoped to avoid when taking on his new responsibilities. Wholehearted team effort seemed important to the future growth of the firm.

Jack Winter has a leadership problem. More specifically, we might say: Jack is not communicating effectively with his managers. Communication! That's the common denominator which threads through most discussions on leadership effectiveness. In fact, the word is used so readily that few of us really stop to consider what it means.

Effective Communication—What Is It?

First and foremost, communication is perception. Prominent management consultant Peter Drucker has observed that communication requires perception. In any dialogue it is the recipient who communicates, not the so-called communicator. In Drucker's words, "The person who emits the communication does not communicate. He utters. Unless there is someone who hears, there is no communication. There is only noise."[2]

Drucker's point is well taken; its implications are rich in meaning for the real estate broker or sales manager concerned about communicating more effectively. Before we can communicate we must know something about the experiences and perceptions of the person to whom we are directing our intended message. To state the point more directly, in communication it is not the message per se, but the interpretation with which it is received that counts.

That perception plays a vital role in the communication process is hardly a new idea. Mary Parker Follett, one of the classical management theorists, observed that conflict or disagreement seldom occurs over substantive solutions to problems.[3] Rather, conflict is most often the result of different perceptions. Each party sees his own aspect of reality and, consequently, the arguments of each seem impertinent to the other.

Demonstrating the role perception plays is not difficult. Picture a large sheet of paper on an easel. This paper is divided into squares (similar to that illustrated in Exhibit 1). I have often hung such a sheet at the front of a classroom and have asked management students to determine how many squares are in the figure. When asked to *individually* determine the number of squares, the answers range from 18 to 54. Working in *pairs*, however, the range typically narrows to 38–42. The majority of the pairs get the correct answer, which is 40. Asked why they improved on their original answers, the usual response is "my partner looked at it differently and saw squares I didn't." Beyond demonstrating that selective perception is commonplace, another lesson is learned. By understanding and utilizing the perceptions of others, our own decisions are often improved. Regardless, unless we understand the percep-

Exhibit 1
How Many Squares?

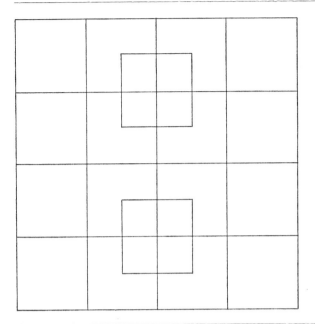

tions of others we are not in a position to present our arguments so that they will be heard.

Communication with others is accomplished most effectively by learning as much as possible about what others think and feel before expressing one's own point of view. Most managers fail to communicate effectively because, very simply, they talk too much. Truly effective communicators are skilled in drawing people out, listening to and interpreting what they hear. Only then do they present their own opinions, incorporating their newfound understanding of the other person's point of view. In so doing, they make it easier for the other people to receive their message, to really *communicate* with them.

This advice is more easily given than practiced. Since the emergence of the human relations school of management in the 1930s, listening has been a cornerstone of managerial communication. However, for the listening approach to work, two sets of skills need to be utilized: *verbal skill* in drawing people out and *conceptual skill* in interpreting what one hears. All too often the former has been emphasized while the latter suffers from neglect. Yet, listening clearly presupposes that the listener will understand the message being sent.

Understanding Others

Communication experts have long recognized that an effective listener must be capable of understanding what he is hearing. If the listener hears the words but misses the meaning of the other person's comments, he is likely to respond in an inappropriate manner. Such misinterpretation is at the heart of many boss—subordinate conflicts and poor personnel decisions in organizations.

Indeed, one of the things which regularly makes an impression on management consultants is the frequency with which two individuals talk *at* one another while each is in a fundamentally different conversation. A principal cause of this phenomenon was emphasized in the famous Hawthorne Studies more than fifty years ago.[4] In conversation with others, one must distinguish between *statements of fact* and *statements of sentiment or feeling*.

Statements of fact make reference to events, characteristics or conditions which are observable and capable of independent verification. Statements of sentiment or feeling refer to the subjective opinions of the individual; beliefs which are rooted in cultural and personal experiences.

Fact v. Sentiment For purposes of illustration, let's consider the following hypothetical example. If Tom comments that he is cold, and Frank, looking at the thermostat, states that it is 75° in the office, they are essentially talking about two different things. Tom is making a statement of sentiment; he feels cold. Frank is responding with a statement of fact: "It is 75° in the office." The facts do not refute Tom's feeling cold although Frank may think that they should. If Tom persists in claiming he feels cold, Frank is likely to suggest that he is being illogical. How can Tom insist he is cold when the office is already 75°? Frank is likely to wonder. Should the exchange reach this point, we have a communication problem rooted in the fact that Tom and Frank are not in the same conversation.

Our hypothetical illustration has parallels with other, more common office conflicts. "Our commission schedule is unfair" or "Floor time is unevenly distributed" or "I am never told about the really good listings" are examples. The sales manager who responds with facts about the industry commission structure or the percentage of floor time worked by each associate or how a certain listing was handled is countering sentiment with facts. As often as not, he is missing the point. A complaint about commissions or floor time may in reality have little to do with these things. Instead, they can be rationalizations for a poor month. Or perhaps an in-law just received a big promotion and is buying a new house. Maybe the car just broke down. Such occurrences are the lifeblood of sentiments.

The first step the broker must take in establishing communication in situations of this nature is not just to listen, but to understand. Does the sales associate want information (facts) or is he expressing sentiment? As we have seen, sentiment can have little to do with the facts of the situation under discussion. Comments made in an irritated or complaining manner almost always involve sentiment. In such instances what is being communicated is that the other person is upset; the source of his discontent might be something quite removed from the specific complaint. And often the sentiment has been building for some time.

Under such circumstances providing the salesperson with more information will not solve the communication problem. This is not because he is being illogical about the situation. The situation is *inherently non-logical,* meaning the source of the sentiment is subjective experience. Throughout this book, we will see specific illustrations of the role sentiment plays in the communication process. Recognizing when a statement is based on sentiment is an important communication skill, one which can help a sales manager avoid unnecessary conflict.

As will be seen in later chapters, establishing communication when an issue involves sentiment requires that the manager first help the other person to clarify the sentiment in his own mind. Once this happens the other person is more likely to be prepared to deal with relevant facts.

Developing the verbal skills necessary for doing this is an important objective of this book. For now, it is sufficient that the reader understand the distinction between statements of fact and of sentiment, and learn to recognize them during conversation.

Jack Winter
Revisited

We left Jack Winter with a problem: how he should react to the apparent lack of cooperation from his office managers.

It is possible for us to speculate about how the branch managers responded to Jack's directive. To be pessimistic about the matter, possibly their sentiments got in the way of the logic of purchasing efficiencies. This would be understandable. Jack was limiting (perhaps perceived as usurping) a traditional prerogative of the branch managers. Since managers usually have strong egos, not to mention a well-developed sense of status, most often they strive for increased, not reduced, authority. Typically, actions which circumscribe their discretionary powers arouse feelings of resentment and resistance.

There are, of course, other elements of Jack's situation which could reinforce this reaction on the part of the managers. Probably he was a rival of some of the managers who perceive his promotion as a loss for them. To such individuals his directive was likely to be perceived as "Jack throwing his weight around." Further, despite his outstanding track record, he is in a new job, the limits of which are still somewhat unclear. For the managers, then, this directive might represent a test case for establishing how they are going to deal with this new position of sales director.

If any or all of the above are true, through their lack of response the branch managers are sending Jack a message. After all, *people do not always communicate by saying something. Many times what a person does not say or do communicates more than what he does.* In this case, their inaction is saying "We are upset." "We do not agree with this policy."

On the other hand, perhaps the branch managers have not had occasion to respond. Maybe the new directive motivated them to be more prudent in their purchases.

Then again, perhaps the seriousness of the situation exists only within the perception of Jack's mind. Maybe he is a victim of *his own* sentiments. This analysis would suggest that

a. because the managers have not sent in any purchasing requests, Jack *assumes* they are resisting him.
b. he *feels* angry toward the managers because they are threatening his concept of himself as a good manager.
c. he *perceives* them as being disrespectful or rebellious.

This line of reasoning can easily lead to Jack's taking some kind of inappropriate, authoritative action.

There is one obvious fact about this situation. Neither Jack nor we know what is going through the minds of the branch managers. The first step has to be dialogue, generated by Jack visiting the branch managers to discuss their situations. In fact, the argument can be made that Jack should have done that before sending out his directive. This is a situation in which sentiment would predictably play a role. And sentiment generally does not respond well to the logic of efficiency as expressed in memos.

A Word On Written Communications

This is primarily a book on handling verbal, face-to-face encounters. However, written communication is an important part of managing and what is written (and how it is written) often shapes the direction of our interpersonal encounters.

The case of Jack Winter contains an important lesson on the role of written communication in the real estate office. Essentially written documents *inform,* but they do not necessarily communicate. As we have suggested above, what is communicated is what the other person reads into the memo.

This is not to suggest that written documents are not important. Indeed, they are invaluable. For example, every firm should have a policy and procedures manual.[5] Such manuals are the most direct method of informing people how certain situations are to be handled. A well-written policy and procedures manual becomes a point of reference for resolving conflicts and disagreements. In a sense policies and procedures are to organizations what habits are to people. They lead to predictability and consistency of actions.

However, because someone reads a manual does not mean he understands it. Further, because of sentiment, simply referring a person to the manual does not necessarily resolve a point of conflict. Written policies and procedures are the skeleton of real estate office communication; interpersonal relationships are the flesh and muscle. Neither can work without the other.

Similarly, a memo or letter is often the most expedient way of informing someone of something. It is generally the poorest method of eliciting cooperation. And cooperation is the lifeline of administration. No broker can communicate personally with every person in the firm on every issue. However, when cooperation is necessary and a decision affects the traditional relationships or work habits of the people involved, direct, personal communication is often the only effective method of obtaining agreement.

It is amazing how often real estate managers will get this backward. Their sales meetings are consumed by giving people detailed information, while decisions which affect their prerogatives (à la Jack Winter) or might improve their performance are communicated by memo. For example, one broker's agenda reveals that his

Monday morning meetings include much discussion of items such as changes in interest rates and lists of "for sale by owners," information which could easily be passed on in written form. However, tips on sales techniques, which are often best learned through role-play in a group setting, are communicated in photocopies of articles circulated through the office.

Communication Within the Sales Office

Communication is understanding. For the REALTOR® this means being able to get ideas across in a manner understandable to the staff. Doing so implies knowing the feelings and needs of the members of the firm. A simple idea, perhaps, but one which is alarmingly elusive in practice.

I am thinking of a midwestern broker who seemed to have one of the most promising firms in his area. Short-term growth of his firm had been rapid and he began to open branch offices.

Currently, this same broker has a three-person office. His best people have joined other firms. Twice this pattern has repeated itself. Essentially, his former associates concede he is a victim of his own poor communication.

The real estate sales office offers an interesting case study in communication. Virtually every sales manager or broker has already demonstrated that he can communicate effectively in one type of business situation: sales. In today's increasingly sophisticated marketplace, the professional sales associate understands that communicating with prospects requires work. Selling is more than just idle conversation. Obtaining listings, getting leads, showing houses effectively—all these activities involve highly developed communication skills. Yet, an individual who is very successful in communicating with sellers and buyers may fail to transfer these skills into the management situation.

Yet the smart broker realizes that the key to building a successful and expanding business is to be as effective in communicating with staff as with clients. Both represent an important part of the business.

The purpose of this book is to help brokers and sales managers develop interpersonal communication skills useful in managing their sales and clerical support staff more effectively. Practical methods—not theory—for managing others are provided.

Using these methods requires skill. Where appropriate, exercises specifically designed to provide practice in the methods and techniques discussed in the chapter are provided. These are to assist the interested reader in skill development. Skill consists of more than memorizing technique; one must become sufficiently comfortable with the technique so that it blends easily with one's own aptitude and style.

The key to developing this kind of skill is practice. Initially, application of the methods may feel awkward. This is true when developing any new skill, whether it's serving a tennis ball, public speaking or selling. Gradually, however, awkwardness gives way to familiarity and application becomes almost automatic.

The skill development process begins with the core communication skills.

Footnotes for Chapter One

1. Robert Katz, "Skills of an Effective Administrator," *Harvard Business Review,* September-October 1974.

2. Peter F. Drucker, "Information, Communications and Understanding." Reprinted in essays by Drucker, *Technology, Management and Society* (New York: Harper & Row, 1970).

3. Mary Parker Follett, *Dynamic Administration* (New York: Harper & Brother, 1941).

4. For an elaboration on the distinction between fact and sentiment, see F. J. Roethlisberger, *Management and Morale* (Cambridge: Harvard University Press, 1941). The late Fritz Roethlisberger was one of the investigators from the Harvard Business School associated with the famous Hawthorne Studies, and a founder of the human relations school of management. Many of his articles on the role of sentiment in communication are considered classics.

5. *Your Policy and Procedure Manual* (Chicago: REALTORS NATIONAL MARKETING INSTITUTE®, 1969).

Chapter 2
Core Communication Skills: Building Blocks For Managerial Effectiveness

Effective managerial communication is built upon a foundation of skills. As with any skill, communication involves the use of specific tools and techniques.

Too often managers fail to realize that communication skills can be developed and improved. Unfortunately the assumption is often made that one is either a born communicator or is not. Certain managers are looked upon as natural communicators; others just don't seem to have the knack for getting their ideas across to others.

To be sure, every now and then a manager comes along who is "a natural." These individuals have a style uniquely their own, not easily imitated. Happily, however, effective communication is an art which can be learned. As is the case with the development of any skill, aptitude plays a part, but with concentrated practice, any broker can become more skilled in communicating with his staff and sales team.

Few of us have been trained how to communicate. From early childhood we are taught how to talk. Communication, of course, involves much more than talking. While we may know how to converse with others, we don't necessarily know the art of getting through to them.

This chapter presents a series of *core* communication skills. They are called core skills because they find wide application in the full range of sensitive and important communication problems which confront any manager. They are presented here as techniques. As we discussed in Chapter 1, skill is more than technique. Skill is the mastery of technique so that it can be purposely and effectively applied toward certain ends.

Managerial communication is purposeful communication. To be successful in building a growing and virile organization, a broker skilled in the techniques discussed in this chapter will have a set of tools which can be selected and applied to improve performance throughout the whole firm.

Consider the variety of managerial communication situations with which a broker or sales manager must deal. Over the course of any given week he must interview applicants in an effort to obtain enough information to make a sound contractual decision on sales personnel, train the staff in effective sales techniques and other job–related skills and practices, mediate conflicts between members of the sales team over such sensitive issues as listings and split commissions, critique the performance of others and terminate individuals who, for one reason or another, are leaving the firm. This abbreviated but representative list illustrates the diverse communication situations which confront the broker.

There are learned approaches, or models, for handling each of the above kinds of situations. Each approach requires a specific blending of the core skills presented below. In other words, development of the core skills is a prerequisite to applying the managerial models suggested in this book.

A professional basketball team with a proud history of championship success recently struggled through a losing season. In postseason interviews the team's management agreed: next season's team had to have players who were well versed in the fundamentals of the game. Without sound fundamentals, the complex patterns of the professional team were lacking in execution. So it is in management. Good fundamental skills are required for effective resolution of the complex situations which confront the professional broker.

The Core Communication Skills

As discussed in Chapter 1, *active listening* has long been a cornerstone piece of advice in communication literature. The rewards of listening—attempting to understand the other person's viewpoint—are many. First, it helps the broker find out what attitudes and underlying problems may exist. Often the reasons or explanations others—such as sales associates and clerical staff—offer are not the true roadblocks to better performance. Rather they are the "safe," reasonable things to say. If the person is encouraged to speak more freely about his feelings, more significant and real issues are likely to emerge. Listening helps the broker avoid attacking the other person's arguments. This reduces defensiveness in both parties and helps them examine things more objectively.

As the term active implies, the listening process is one which can be managed. Several of the core skills are often labeled listening skills. In particular, listening skills include:

1. Questions
2. Expanders
3. Restatement
4. Reflection
5. Silence

Questions

Questions are the most basic tools of effective managerial communication. *The heart of the management process is collecting information.* Regardless of the specific nature of the situation, be it interviewing, resolving conflict, criticizing or problem–solving, the broker must gather information, assess it and decide on a course of action. Reduced to its most common denominator, this is what management is all about. The first step in the process is gathering information. And in interpersonal situations, questions are the basic tools of information gathering.

Everybody asks questions all the time. Unfortunately, we don't always use our questions effectively. As we shall see, there are several types of questions, each of which can accomplish certain communication purposes. In this sense questions represent a series of tools which are available to managerial craftsmen. Indeed, to paraphrase a popular expression, when working with others what you ask determines what you get. In this chapter, we will consider the most basic kinds of questions: open-ended questions, close-ended questions, and directed questions.

Open-ended and Close-ended Questions An open-ended question is a question which cannot be easily answered yes or no. Open-ended questions are begun with the words: what, how, where, who or when.

In contrast, close-ended questions are easily answered in a yes or no fashion. Close-ended questions typically begin with the words: can, have, do, did, are, has, would, could.

Exhibit 2
Phrasing Questions

Words which phrase open-ended questions	Words which phrase close-ended questions
How	Did
What	Do
Who	Can
When	Have
Where	Don't
	Would
	Could
	Are
	Won't
	Will
	Is

Because open-ended questions cannot be easily answered yes or no, they generally elicit more information. For example, asking a sales associate, "How did you qualify the prospect?" requires more extensive explanation than "Did you qualify the prospect?" To answer the former, the sales associate has to respond with an explanation.

Apart from generating a broader response, open-ended questions minimize defensiveness on the part of the other person. Close-ended questions tend to force the other person into a position of deciding whether they wish to come down on the positive or negative side of the yes/no question. This decision can be threatening. It certainly influences the kind of information which is offered. Open-ended questions make it easier for the other person to explain their position.

Skilled lawyers are astute in the use of questions. During initial pre-trial interviews they are likely to ask open-ended questions of potential witnesses, questions which provide the other person with considerable latitude in his answers. This latitude increases the likelihood of the attorney picking up unintended clues and information. In court the same attorney can phrase effective close-ended questions, the truthful answers to which can place a witness in a damaging light. The witness finds the question, although direct, difficult to answer and express accurately what really happened. Such questions serve to censor certain aspects of what happened which the attorney wishes to avoid having come out in court.

For these reasons, open-ended questions are generally more effective during the exploration stage of a sensitive discussion when a REALTOR® is attempting to understand what has happened. By using open-ended questions the broker is more likely to gather important information while avoiding unnecessary defensiveness.

Unfortunately, most questions which get asked in our society are close-ended. Listen to the questions which get asked during conversations in the office! Most of them are phrased in a close-ended fashion. This is fine for casual conversation, but it often gets us into problems when involved in touchy managerial situations. There are very few close-ended questions which could not be phrased in an open-ended fashion. Unfortunately, our habit of asking close-ended questions often makes this a difficult skill to develop. Exercise 2-A at the end of this chapter will give you some practice in phrasing open-ended questions.

Because of the tendency to use close-ended questions where open-ended ones would be more appropriate, we are placing more emphasis on the latter. Open-ended questions are especially useful in handling conflict situations, dealing with expressions of sentiment, collecting assessment information and other critical and difficult managerial tasks. This is not to suggest that close-ended questions are very useful when the broker is trying to elicit specific answers. Remember *close-ended questions tend to restrict, constrain and focus the flow of information, while open-ended questions have the opposite effect.*

Avoiding "Why" Questions Especially early in a conversation it is best for the broker to avoid questions which begin with "Why". "Why" obviously phrases an open-ended question. However, in our language, "Why" carries the connotation, "Justify yourself." It implies fault. Therefore, repeated, "Why" questions tend to get excuses rather than explanations.

This happens all the time with our children. We ask our child, "Johnny, why did you hit Billy?" You can almost see Johnny's eyes go up into his head as he thinks to himself, "Let's see, what answer will Dad buy?" A better way of asking the question would have been "What happened?"

Fault is a concept which is useful in legal proceedings, but which often gets in the way of management communication. Therefore, the broker wants to ask questions which tend to establish fault only when it is important for him to do so. Otherwise, it is more important to learn "what happened." When coaching members of the staff, the broker usually wants an explanation so alternative methods of dealing with similar situations in the future can be developed. Fault is really irrelevant. The event happened. The issue is how to prevent a recurrence, not to get a confession and exact punishment. "Why" questions introduce the specter of fault.

Once again, our habits are likely to get in the way of effective communication. When we do ask an open-ended question, it tends to begin with "Why." In developing skill in using open-ended questions, the broker needs to be sensitive to the uses of "Why" questions.

Directed or Linking Questions A directed question is one which relates directly to an earlier comment made by the other person. It contains a word or phrase the person used and essentially asks for further amplification. Usually it will be phrased in an open-ended fashion. An example is:

Sales Associate: That certainly *puzzled* me.
Broker: What aspects were particularly puzzling to you?

Asking directed questions is the key to making progress in a tough communication situation. When brokers first try to use open-ended questions as a communication tool, many times they feel they are spinning their wheels. Observation usually reveals that they appear to be playing a game of Twenty Questions with the staff member, asking surface questions and not probing to learn what really happened.

While broad–brush open-ended questions can get the conversation going, as much as possible the broker must tie subsequent questions into the sales associate's previous answers.

Expanders

Beyond asking questions, there are other things a broker can do to relax the salesperson and facilitate the exchange of information. One of these things is the use of expanders. Expanders are gestures and verbal expressions which communicate interest and understanding in what the other person is saying.

Nodding the head, good eye contact, and such common phrases as: "uh-huh," "ummm-hummm" and "I see" are all examples of expanders. Psychologists refer to these gestures as expanders because they tend to encourage people to expand on their answers.

When we ask other people questions, especially about sensitive issues, they are often hesitant to answer. Expanders serve to relax the person and encourage him to elaborate on his answer.

We have all seen expanders work. If you have ever given a speech and you do not like to talk in front of groups, I'll bet the following happened. You found at least one person in the audience who was nodding his head in agreement and by the end of the speech you were talking mostly to him. Why? Because his nodding was interpreted by you as interest in what you were saying. This tended to put you at ease.

Of course, the broker should avoid over-using these gestures since they would then come across as insincere. But occasional use of expanders reinforces the other person, making him more likely to volunteer important information.

Restatement

Restatement is the most difficult of the core skills to develop. It is also one of the most effective. Restatement is the process of taking what has been said to you by another person and saying it back to him or her, relating it in a brief or summarized form. It is a very powerful tool for exploring the feelings and opinions of others.

Restatement works because it is based on one of the most widespread human needs—the need to be understood. When we repeat or restate what another individual is saying to us, we send a clear and unmistakable message to him that we *have*, in fact, listened and understood what was said. When the other person hears his own thoughts coming back, it very often creates a desire in him to tell us even more. As well as elaborating on his ideas and opinions, the other person may alter or adjust his thoughts somewhat. Restatement, in effect, permits the other person to react to his own ideas.

Phrases like "you feel," "you think," "you believe," "in other words, you. . ." are often helpful starters for restating what a person said. For example:

Commercial Sales Manager:
> The business plan may look good on paper, but I just don't think it will work.

Broker:
> You feel it has some flaws.

Commercial Sales Manager:
> Well, not really flaws. I just don't think these calculations make sense.

Broker:
> You believe we've made some errors in our figures.

Commercial Sales Manager:
> Not really errors; I don't think you've taken into consideration that the Boston office has two new men in it. They're not experienced enough to put together some of the deals you are assuming.

Now the broker knows what the sales manager really meant when he indicated, "I don't think it will work."

Caution in Use of Restatement Brokers often express concern, when first learning to listen by restating that it will be unnatural, that it might sound unreal or phony. These fears are justified if a sincere desire to listen is not the case. In such instances, salespeople will often feel that they are being "techniqued." It cannot be overstated that the tools presented here will only be effective when the broker is *sincerely interested in the other person's point of view.*

Restating will not work if the broker restates something that was too matter-of-fact; something that was not sensitive, conflict laden or otherwise of personal interest to the other person. For example:

Office Manager:
> I'll have these reports ready for you two days ahead of schedule.

Broker:
> The reports will be ready before we planned.

Office Manager:
> Yeah, that's right.

Remember, *restatement works best when the other person is intensely interested or feels strongly about the point they are making.* This means that timing is important. With practice, however, timing will become almost intuitive.

Developing Skill in Restating In addition to restating at the appropriate time, it is important to restate properly. Restating requires the broker to listen very carefully to what the other person is saying. And, it requires the ability to extract the essence of what is being said and put it in slightly different words. Merely *repeating* what the other person has said won't be effective. For example:

Salesperson:
> This prospect doesn't know what he wants!

Broker:	Your prospect doesn't know what he wants.
Salesperson:	(*With a queer look on his face*) Yeah, that's what I said.

When you have time, try your hand at Exercise 2-B at the end of this chapter. It will get you started in practicing restatement.

Reflection

Reflection is similar to restatement. Restatement has to do with the *content* of what a person said, while reflection has to do with the *feeling* expressed. In reflection the broker expresses the emotion which seems to be underlying the other person's comments.

This is valuable because it encourages the person to discuss his feelings, getting them off his chest. Strongly felt emotions are a major block to open communication. Also, because reflection conveys real understanding, the other person is more likely to be willing to examine the source of his feelings with the broker. Thus reflection can help the broker handle conversation marked with sentiment. Since the other person feels the broker already appreciates his feelings, he is encouraged to share his difficulties. A question will not usually do this. For instance:

Broker:	How's the new deal coming along?
Commercial Salesperson:	
	(*Said in a somewhat discouraged tone*) Oh, it's coming along okay.
Broker:	Are you discouraged about your progress on the project?
Commercial Salesperson:	
	Oh, no. We're coming along with it all right.

Now notice the difference when *reflection* is used rather than *questions:*

Broker:	How's the new deal coming along?
Commercial Salesperson:	
	(*Discouraged tone*) Oh, it's coming along okay.
Broker:	It can get discouraging during the early stages of a complex deal.
Commercial Salesperson:	
	You know, I didn't want to say anything, but yesterday, I was talking with the lawyers and ...

Note that in the second example, the salesperson can share his problem with the broker. He shares his worry because he is not put on the spot by a question that requires a potentially embarrassing answer. But, more important, he knows the broker knows he's a little down. Since the broker already seems to understand his problem and is not reacting negatively, the salesperson is willing to open up and explore it.

Silence

One of the most powerful tools in any broker's repertoire of listening skills is silence. Whenever two people are engaged in a conversation and a pause occurs, tremendous psychological pressure is built up. This is one of the reasons why the pause technique works. Silence asks, without the use of words, what else can you add? There is a certain implication in silence that suggests more is expected.

Silence may not initially strike the reader as a skill. But its effective use during communication requires as much skill as any of the other techniques we have discussed.

The use of silence carries with it the inherent problem of threat. Silence can be misused and abused. When this occurs, it tends to reduce the free flow of conversation rather than encourage it.

There are, though, two occasions when silence can be used effectively without attendant threat or discomfort. The first is right after the broker has asked a question. Think about what typically happens when we ask another person a question and they don't respond right away. What happens? We are inclined to somehow clarify the question or to jump in and answer the question ourself, or ask another question. Any of these reactions defeats the purpose of asking questions in the first place.

When a question is addressed to someone, it is clearly understood by the one questioned that it is his turn to speak. There is no real justification to continue talking once you have asked a question. If the other person wants to break the tension of silence, he can always do so with a statement such as: "Would you mind re-phrasing your question?" or "I am not sure what you mean."

Whenever a question is asked and the other person doesn't respond, it most likely means the other person is thinking about what to say. Beautiful! That's one of the reasons we ask questions: to get the other person thinking about the issues involved. To be able to ask a good question and shut up is truly a communication skill.

Know When to Shut Up Make yourself conscious of how often you ask questions of others and then go on to suggest an answer. Practice phrasing a good question and then keeping quiet.

Short pauses are also helpful when the other person has been talking and we would like them to continue. Sometimes the most effective thing we can do is to pause and look expectant. Almost always the other person will continue talking.

Interestingly, it is after such a pause that the other person is most likely to reveal a sensitive or embarrassing problem. What happens is that even as he is talking he is thinking to himself: "He seems to understand." "How much should I tell him?" He stops talking—you pause instead of commenting—and it comes out. For example:

Broker:	How can we make more certain you meet your sales objectives this quarter?
Salesperson:	I guess the main thing should be to set a list of priorities for each day.
Broker:	*(pause for 5-6 seconds)*
Salesperson:	You know, sometimes you are so busy with your own selling that you are never around to answer questions. That makes it kind of tough, too.

Applying the Listening Skills We have learned five listening skills, each of which facilitate a communication process:

- Questions
- Expanders
- Restatement
- Reflection
- Silence

All these techniques are ways of listening and helping members of your staff to think out loud along with you. In most instances, they are non-threatening and convey an interest in what the other person is saying. And most importantly, they are methods of gathering information.

By using listening skills instead of attacking or arguing with the other person, you reduce his need to put up further defenses. In such instances, he is also very likely to examine his excuses and rationalizations and recognize them for what they are. In other words, the other person begins to explore the problem. Here is a typical example:

Broker:	Mary, this is the third time this week you have been late.
Salesperson:	Well, I couldn't really help it with this bad weather and snow. I've been held up in traffic. It's terrible.
Broker:	Let's see what you're saying here ... the reason you've been late these past few mornings is the traffic tie-ups. What other delay might you have encountered? (Note: the broker did not attack Mary's excuses, even though he was tempted to say, "Well, Mary, I drove almost the same route and made it here on time—the traffic wasn't that bad.")
Salesperson:	Well, it's kinda tough getting out of the house on time ... it's not always easy.
Broker:	(*Trying to understand and listen further*) Some things at home in the morning make it difficult. (*Pause*)
Salesperson:	I didn't want to say anything, but (*pause*) well frankly, I've got a few problems with my husband.
Broker:	It's something that's difficult for you to talk about.
Salesperson:	I guess I might as well tell you ... my husband has a real drinking problem.

In the above dialogue the broker has used communication skills to avoid creating a conflict between himself and the salesperson. Instead, he is making progress toward identifying the problem. We will learn more about how to handle these situations in Chapters 3 and 4. But first we have to learn another core communication skill.

Raising Sensitive Points—Be Descriptive, Not Evaluative

Listening is only part of the communication process. The broker also has to be able to get his points across to the other person. For example, listening is not always totally effective in overcoming someone else's defensiveness. At times the broker has to provide illustrations of what he is talking about to get the other person to examine a problem.

Additionally, if the broker has observed something he wants corrected, the onus is on him to raise the issue with the other person.

Trying to get the other person to bring it up by asking roundabout questions like "How do you think you did with that prospect?" when the broker knows what he wants to talk about is phony and leads to game–playing.

A key skill in getting our points across to others is the ability to state issues *descriptively*, rather than evaluatively. In other words, describe the situation rather than attack the person. Most persons can more objectively discuss their activities and how they actually behaved in certain situations than they can talk about evaluative judgments about themselves. For example, when you say, "Two reports are late," it tends to beget less defensiveness than when you say, "You're careless when it comes to meeting deadlines." Placing a value judgment on something represents more of a personal attack on the other person's ego.

Unfortunately, most criticizing is done in an evaluative and judgmental fashion. This tends to generate an unnecessary level of defensiveness. It also diverts from the real issue since much of the subsequent conversation tends to focus on the evaluation, with the salesperson challenging it and the broker defending it, instead of both trying to solve the problem.

Being descriptive does not eliminate defensiveness but it does reduce it. It also positions the broker to better deal with the other person's defensiveness, since he is focusing on events which have occurred, not judgments about those events.

This suggests another advantage to being descriptive: it helps the broker maintain an open mind for listening. Normally, when another person does something which disturbs us, we make an evaluative judgment in our minds which we communicate directly to the person. Often we make statements which contain words which intensify the evaluative effect—words such as poor, lousy, ineffective or unacceptable. In being descriptive the broker is focusing his own attention on what actually happened instead of on his subjective reaction to it. Having made an evaluative statement, the broker is placed in a position of having to defend his judgment. A descriptive statement in effect places the broker in a position of having said, "That's what I observed; now help me figure out what it means." Here are some examples:

Evaluative	*Descriptive*
You aren't motivated to succeed	You have missed your scheduled floor time four times this month.

You commercial guys are uncooperative	Tom told me he hasn't heard from you yet on that lead I gave you.
You don't plan well.	When you plan, I notice you do it on a weekly basis but do not work out a monthly list of priorities.
You did a poor job of conducting the sales meeting this morning.	I want to talk with you about the meeting this morning when the sales staff began directing their questions to me rather than you.
You don't communicate well with your prospects.	When you talk with your prospects you often cut them off in the middle of their sentences.

Being descriptive is not being roundabout or indirect, nor is it an attempt to pull punches. Rather, a descriptive statement is direct, specific and to the point without attributing cause or motive to the situation.

There are sound communication reasons for doing this. Primary among them is that an evaluative statement is based on our *perception* of what happened. As we learned in the first chapter, our perceptions can lead us to some less than accurate conclusions. For example, consider the situation in the illustrative dialogue about Mary not getting to work on time which concluded our discussion of listening skills. It would have been easy to arrive at an initial judgment that Mary was irresponsible or didn't care about getting to work. Yet, the real problem centered around her husband's drinking problem at home.

Guidelines for Phrasing Descriptive Statements The key to being descriptive is to present what actually occurred. Four guideline questions for doing this are:

1. *What did the broker actually see or hear?* i.e., setting weekly targets, but no monthly priorities, cutting others off in mid-sentence, arriving late for work.
2. *How often has the behavior been observed?* i.e., twice, three times, frequently.

3. *Who was involved?* i.e., just the salesperson, several prospects, other members of the staff.
4. *What were the observable consequences?* i.e., paperwork is building up, listings are down, a prospect walks out.

Not every descriptive statement will answer all four questions. However, to the extent the broker's statements do contain the answers to these questions, it is likely he is being descriptive.

For example, Harriet, a broker in the Southwest, felt one of her sales associates tended to be condescending with prospects. Of course, to say "You're condescending" would be both evaluative and not very helpful. After all, how does one set out to be less condescending?

Harriet asked herself, what does this person actually do which strikes me as condescending? One thing Harriet observed was that when someone else had an idea the sales associate always seemed to have a better one. She would also tend to focus on the bad points of the suggestions of others and never focus on any positive things. Harriet had seen this happen with several prospects and on a couple of occasions the prospect began acting frustrated.

Harriet now knew how to raise the issue in a descriptive fashion. "Mary, in your dealings with prospects, I've noticed that when they make a suggestion you either come up with a better one or right away tell them why it won't work. Sometimes they act upset about this, like the time Mr. Franklin said, 'Well, it's my money.' "

As with the listening skills, phrasing things descriptively takes practice. At first it seems awkward. However, in time it will seem almost automatic.

To start practicing, try Exercise 2-C at the end of the chapter.

Conclusion

In this chapter we have learned some core communication skills. They are useful in a wide range of situations. Becoming skilled in their use requires practice and patience. Don't expect immediate success. Remember how long it takes to develop certain motor skills like serving a tennis ball or driving a golf ball. And even with practice we aren't always on target. Communication skills are similar. But developing them is basic to becoming a professional manager just as you teach your salespeople to practice their selling skills.

The next couple of chapters deal with more complex communication models, but in them you will find applications for these core skills; the building blocks of managerial effectiveness.

Exercise 2-A
Practice in Phrasing Open-ended Questions

Below are eight close-ended questions. In the space below each question, rewrite the question in an open-ended fashion. On the following page some possible answers are provided. Remember, the purpose of an open-ended question is to encourage the other person to express himself.

1. Do you like the idea of transferring to the Simsbury office?

_____

_____

_____

2. Don't you see the advantage of this procedure change?

_____

_____

_____

3. Does Fred's idea sound like a good one to you?

_____

_____

_____

4. Will you help out this afternoon?

_____

_____

_____

5. Can you see any advantages to this idea?

_____

_____

_____

6. Are you worried about the new sales associate?

_____

_____

_____

7. Could you help Don over in the closing department?

_____

_____

_____

8. Have you received the necessary secretarial support?

_____

_____

_____

_____

Exercise 2-A
Possible Answers

Open-ended questions begin with: How, What, Where, Who, When.

1. Do you like the idea of transferring to the Simsbury office?
   a. What are your feelings about transferring to Simsbury?
   b. How do you feel about transferring to Simsbury?

2. Don't you see the advantage of this procedure change?
   a. What advantages do you see to the procedure change?
   b. Where do you see advantages to changing the procedures?

3. Does Fred's idea sound like a good one to you?
   a. What do you like about Fred's idea?
   b. Where do you think Fred's idea might help us?

4. Will you help out this afternoon?
   a. How much can you help out this afternoon?
   b. When will you be able to help out this afternoon?

5. Can you see any advantages to this idea?
   a. What advantages do you see to this idea?
   b. How do you see this idea helping us?

6. Are you worried about the new sales associate?
   a. What concerns do you have about the new sales associate?
   b. What is there about the new sales associate that worries you?

7. Could you help Don over in the closing department?
   a. What help can you give Don over in the closing department?
   b. How do you think you might help Don in the closing department?

8. Have you received the necessary secretarial support?
   a. What secretarial support have you received?
   b. How well has the secretarial staff been supporting you?

Exercise 2-B
Practice in Restatement

Below are some statements which might be made by another person. In the space provided fill in how you would restate what they are saying. Remember these comments are taken out of context. Try to imagine they are part of a conversation the other person feels strongly about.

Be careful not to write in questions. The purpose of this exercise is to restate. Possible restatements are found on the following page.

1. (*Other person*) Well, I just don't know whether the staff will accept these changes.

   (*Your restatement*) _____

   _____

2. (*Other person*) Sometimes he just isn't very receptive to our suggestions.

   (*Your restatement*) _____

   _____

3. (*Other person*) The salespeople were not very happy with the outcome of yesterday's meeting.

   (*Your restatement*) _____

   _____

4. I am worried we won't make the deadline.

   (*Your restatement*) _____

   _____

5. There's a lot of merit in what you are saying, but there are some problems, too!

   (*Your restatement*) _____

   _____

6. He really likes the service we have given him.

   (*Your restatement*) _____

Exercise 2-B
Possible Answers

1. Well, I just don't know whether the staff will accept these changes.
   - *You feel the staff might resist some of these changes.*

2. Sometimes he just isn't very receptive to our suggestions.
   - *He doesn't always respond well to our ideas.*

3. The salespeople were not very happy with the outcome of yesterday's meeting.
   - *The meeting didn't turn out the way they expected.*

4. I am worried we won't make the deadline.
   - *You feel there's a chance we won't get done on time.*

5. There's a lot of merit in what you are saying, but there are some problems, too!.
   - *You see some problems with my suggestions.*

6. He really likes the service we have given him.
   - *He's pleased with our service.*

Exercise 2-C
Practice in Writing Descriptive Statements

Below are some typical evaluative comments. Think about instances when you've made this kind of evaluative judgment about someone's performance. Using this situation as a reference, write a descriptive statement in the space provided.

Examples of descriptive statements are found on the following page.

Evaluative: You are too disorganized.

Descriptive: _____

_____

_____

Evaluative: You did not handle that prospect well.

Descriptive: _____

_____

_____

Evaluative: Sometimes you come across somewhat condescendingly.

Descriptive: _____

_____

_____

Evaluative: You are not aggressive enough.

Descriptive: _____

_____

_____

Exercise 2-C
Possible Descriptive Statements

Evaluative: You are too disorganized.
Descriptive: When you go to meetings you often forget important papers.

Evaluative: You did not handle that prospect well.
Descriptive: Several times when the prospect asked questions you told him not to worry about that. His look suggested to me he felt you were ducking the question.

Evaluative: Sometimes you come across somewhat con-descendingly.
Descriptive: I have noticed you often tell prospects that their concerns are not that important.

Chapter 3
Managing Conflict: Dealing With the Tough Communication Problems

Many real estate sales managers repeatedly ask, "How do I avoid conflict in the office?" The answer is, you don't. Rather, you learn how to manage it. Once a broker begins to build an organization (as opposed to a small collection of people), conflict becomes inevitable. In fact, a strong case can be made for the viewpoint that resolving conflict is a central part of any manager's job. Good managers have effective conflict management skills and their organizations benefit from their skill in this area.

Conflict can, of course, be minimized. Sound staff selection procedures, thorough training, regular performance appraisal of office staff and salespeople, and clearly documented policies and procedures can reduce the frequency and intensity of interpersonal conflict. But these management practices won't eliminate it. So accept the fact: willingness to address conflict is a key characteristic of effective management.

The Organizational Roots of Conflict

As a sales organization grows in size, it becomes more complex. Casual face-to-face contact is no longer sufficient to insure effective staff communication. Complexity is usually managed by introducing formal controls, procedures, and other managerial changes which create tensions for people who must work under them. This relationship between growth, organizational practices and communication has been well documented by Professor Larry E. Greiner of the University of Southern California.[1] The message for the broker with a growing firm is direct: anticipate the predictable problems and plan for them.

Further, as a firm grows it becomes more diversified. New offices are opened in other towns. Sometimes these new offices are located in different residential markets, serving new and different clienteles. Under such conditions, salespeople in the different offices are likely to evolve self-images which reflect the particular market they serve. Colleagues in other branches become perceived as different and if the situation is not well-managed, unfortunate gulfs emerge between offices.

Additionally, growth usually brings expansion in the non-sales areas of the business. Closing and accounting departments grow in size. A business manager may be hired. These administrative employees are likely to have attitudes and job priorities that are different from the sales organization.

To summarize the above, the natural consequences of success weave the potential for conflict into the organizational fabric of a growing firm. Managing this potential for conflict is the most challenging of communication problems.

Conflict Management and Managerial Style

Robert Blake and Jane Mouton are two behavioral scientists whose research into leadership style has made monumental contributions to our understanding of the management process.[2] In particular, Blake and Mouton have developed a method of describing leadership style known as the Managerial Grid®. The grid is especially useful as a way of thinking about the relationship between conflict resolution and management style.

The grid classifies a manager's style along two dimensions: 1) degree of concern for production and 2) degree of concern for people. A high degree of concern on one of the dimensions receives a score of nine, medium concern a score of five and low concern scores one. When the two dimensions are placed against each other, as illustrated in Exhibit 3, a grid emerges. Any manager's style can be categorized by one of five possible points on the grid, depending on his score on each of the dimensions. Interestingly, the styles of individual managers tend to be characterized by certain traits according to where they score on the grid.

Exhibit 3
The Managerial Grid

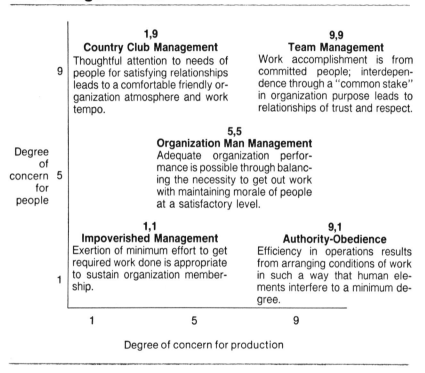

	1,9 **Country Club Management** Thoughtful attention to needs of people for satisfying relationships leads to a comfortable friendly organization atmosphere and work tempo.	9,9 **Team Management** Work accomplishment is from committed people; interdependence through a "common stake" in organization purpose leads to relationships of trust and respect.
Degree of concern for people	5,5 **Organization Man Management** Adequate organization performance is possible through balancing the necessity to get out work with maintaining morale of people at a satisfactory level.	
	1,1 **Impoverished Management** Exertion of minimum effort to get required work done is appropriate to sustain organization membership.	9,1 **Authority-Obedience** Efficiency in operations results from arranging conditions of work in such a way that human elements interfere to a minimum degree.

Degree of concern for production

Five Management Styles

9,1 Style This manager, who scores high in concern for production and low in concern for people, is often characterized by others as having an autocratic approach to his people. The 9,1 manager closely supervises the work of his people, frequently giving directions and making almost all decisions himself. This style of manager focuses on the immediate problem at hand, generally making snap decisions and worrying about tomorrow later. When he approves departures from existing procedures or takes shortcuts in doing something it is usually to improve his number one priority, production.

1,9 Style The opposite of the 9,1 style, the 1,9 manager scores high on concern for people, low on concern for production. Frequently labeled "country club" managers, individuals who fall into this category tend to give too much leeway to their people. In fact, at times they almost abdicate their managerial responsibilities. 1,9 managers will often describe their job as "keeping others satisfied" or comment, "A happy office is a productive office." When this manager bends the rules, it is usually to give his people a break. As the reader has undoubtedly surmised, discipline is not tightly enforced by the 1,9 manager.

1,1 Style Characterized by a low score on both the production and people dimensions, this manager is most conerned with just "getting by." The 1,1 manager does exactly what he is told and no more. The manager sticks by the rules and procedures in order to minimize his exposure and personal accountability. He almost never makes exceptions to established firm practices, regardless of the reasons.

5,5 Style This is a compromise style. The 5,5 manager perceives himself as having to balance his concern for production with a concern for his people. Often the 5,5 manager will discuss some decision he made which was popular with his people as "building up human relations capital which he might need to draw on at some future point." At times he will emphasize production for a while, then let up to give his people a break. For him, management is a series of tradeoffs which have to be made. When making a decision, the 5,5 manager often relies on precedent or how a situation has been handled in the past.

9,9 Style The 9,9 style is a consultative problem solver who attempts to get top production by actively involving his people in the problems of the business. Placing a strong emphasis on production, the 9,9 manager views his role as one of strongly supporting the activities of his sales staff.

Blake and Mouton's studies demonstrate that the 9,9 manager is most likely to build an effective organization capable of sustaining a high level of performance over the long run. In other words, it's the 9,9 manager who is most likely to establish the kind of firm that attracts and retains top people while becoming a major factor in the local real estate market.

The 5,5 manager is the next most effective, followed by the 9,1, 1,9, and 1,1 styles.

The Styles and Conflict Management

Experienced management consultants are well aware that managers with each of the different styles behave in very distinctive ways on the job. For example, observing a 9,1 manager with a 1,9 is a study in contrasts. However, despite their obvious behavioral differences, 9,1, 1,9, 1,1 and 5,5 managers are alike in one critical respect. All four tend to view conflict negatively believing it to be detrimental to the firm. Further, they tend to assume that the personal interests of their associates are ultimately different from the interests of the firm. The fact that the needs of people are different from the needs of the firm is for these managers the basic source of much of the conflict which exists. What people want and what the firm needs are different and managers are caught in the middle.

Sharing these beliefs, their styles differ in the methods used in dealing with conflict. The 9,1 manager emphasizes production while intimidating his people and ignoring those who leave. He has little concern for why they left. The 1,9 manager adopts the opposite strategy, trying to make people happy and often procrastinating in his dealing with disruptive associates. In the process, the firm suffers. 1,1 managers do it by the book, pleading consistency and precedent when making unpopular decisions. The 5,5 manager searches for opportunities to make trade-offs. Each in his own way is seeking to suppress conflict.

9,9 managers are set apart by their belief that conflict is something which, when effectively confronted and resolved, paves the way for future growth and success. Characterized by the belief that associates should be able to satisfy their personal needs within the firm, the 9,9 manager views conflict as a signal that positive managerial intervention is necessary. Thus, he seeks to address conflict in a positive, consultative fashion.

Cases in Conflict Management

Let's get down to cases. Each of the following situations is representative of the difficult managerial communication problems which confront brokers in growing, successful organizations.

Case Number One: How does a new manager elicit support from the old guard salespeople?

Karen Cassidy has recently been appointed sales director of Harrison Realty, a firm with six offices and $32 million in sales. Harrison Realty was founded by Frank Harrison six years ago to serve a semi-rural New England town and suburban areas. Frank has always placed emphasis on sound management, selecting only full-time associates and putting a high priority on staff development and training. Like many successful entrepreneurs, Frank has a charismatic personality which elicits considerable loyalty from his associates. They attribute a large part of their success to his efforts in developing them. For Frank, the establishment of a sales director is a necessary step to free him from daily involvement with firm operations so he can plan for the future of the organization. Karen's problem is establishing credibility. Many of the office managers bypass Karen to talk with Frank. With Frank having been so intensely involved in the development of his people, it is hard for them to call Karen to discuss their problems because of their respect for Frank. There is also some envy on the part of the other branch managers, each of whom wonder why Karen was selected instead of them.

Further, the associates complain that the firm has lost the family feeling. As one sales associate stated to Frank, "I helped you grow, now I don't know what's happening." As staff members attempt to communicate with Frank, Karen often finds herself spinning her wheels, getting half of a three-way conversation.

Frank is groping for a solution since his effort at retaining the family feeling is undercutting Karen. So far, he has been trying to reinforce Karen's position by making oblique references to the need to deal directly with Karen on matters involving either sales or personnel policy. Frank hopes certain people will get the hint. Time, too, he hopes, will resolve the problem. What should Frank and Karen be doing?

Guidelines for a Solution Assuming Frank has made a good selection, one based on Karen's management potential and not solely her sales record, there were two steps Frank could have taken prior to the announcement of Karen's appointment which would have smoothed the transition. Frank should have met individually with key people who might have wanted the new position, informing them of the decision to promote Karen and explaining why. This would have accomplished a couple of things:

1. Extended to those individuals the courtesy of hearing it first. This would have provided time for them to privately adjust to the new situation as well as communicating Frank's continued appreciation of them.
2. Provided Frank an opportunity to deal with their reactions prior to Karen's official appointment. Since Karen would not have yet assumed her new duties, he could spend time exploring their reaction without running any risk of undercutting Karen.

Second, at the time of the appointment, Frank could have thoroughly explained to the staff not only the need for the new position, which he did, but also the means he would use to keep them informed of developments affecting the firm. Additionally, descriptive illustrations of the kinds of activities Frank will be spending more time on and the advantages of these activities for all concerned should have been given considerable emphasis.

Given the current situation, Frank and Karen must agree to work jointly at resolving the situation. Frank must realize that his own behavior can tend to reinforce the problem with the staff and branch managers. Frank must consciously alter his behavior so that:

1. When associates come to him with a problem he indicates that it is Karen's responsibility to deal with it. If the associate indicates Karen is out of the office, he should ask them to leave a message for her. Remember, there were frequently times in the past when he was out of the office and these issues waited for him. Of course, Frank should explain that if he takes action now it will tangle the lines of communication and might even create a larger problem.
2. If associates come to Frank with a personal complaint about Karen he should ask whether they have talked to Karen about the matter. Only when a problem appears widespread should he become involved and then only after first consulting with Karen.

3. When attending staff meetings, Frank should be sure to let Karen run the meeting. Sales associates and managers will be alert to how many times Frank seems to feel it is necessary to elaborate on Karen's points.

Karen, on the other hand, has to actively manage the situation. The longer Karen allows the situation to continue, the less control she has over the ultimate relationship which will evolve between her and her subordinates. In fact, the odds are that she may never evolve a satisfactory relationship with some key people unless she takes steps to influence the outcome.

First and foremost, Karen needs to remember that *recognition of the needs of others is an important element in creating a supportive climate.* Just as Karen was successful as a sales associate in overcoming the resistance of buyers, she now must understand and creatively meet the personal needs of her subordinates. It is important that she demonstrate understanding and empathy when working with her sales associates. Using the core skills learned in Chapter 2, Karen should be descriptive rather than evaluative when providing subordinates with feedback on their performance. If Karen handles her sales managers and associates in this fashion she will build more cohesive support toward her position. This means Karen must initiate contact with her people, listening to them and identifying ways she can help meet their needs.

Second, Karen must sit down and discuss the situation with any member of her organization who persists in excluding her. Complaining about the problem without confronting the individual involved does nothing to resolve the issue. Further, the longer Karen lets the problem exist, the more difficult it will be to deal with. *Procrastination will build guilt feelings in Karen* since she knows she should confront the issue. Guilt will tend to cause Karen to exaggerate the negative feelings which exist. Plus, *Karen's inaction is giving tacit approval to the other person's behavior.* Oblique references by Frank won't resolve the issue. Only direct action on Karen's part will establish her position as a leader.

What can we learn from this case which may apply in a general way to similar situations? When making a key management change it is important for:

1. The broker or manager initiating the change to
   - anticipate the reactions of others. People do not easily conform to managerial changes. Their emotions become involved.
   - deal with key people on a personal basis *before* the change so that the broker does not have to interfere with the new relationships after the fact.
   - thoroughly explain the benefits of the change.
   - accept that the change is in the long-term interest of the organization and therefore be prepared for some short-term problems.
   - understand that his own behavior following the change will either reinforce or undermine its effectiveness.
2. The new manager to
   - focus on the personal needs of her new subordinates, seeking ways to build bridges of support.
   - deal with any resistance on a direct one-to-one basis as the problem surfaces. Only the new manager can act to establish her own credibility.

Case Number Two: The failing branch manager

Joan Williams joined Triple R Realty three years ago and rapidly emerged as a top producer. When the firm opened a new office in a nearby suburban area, Joan was made the branch manager. The new office was in a highly competitive area, attempting to penetrate a market dominated by old firms with established reputations. However, because Joan was a high achiever, the brokers were optimistic Joan would develop a good, profitable office.

Within six months, it was clear the new office was in trouble. Sales were significantly below expectations. The phone seldom rang. Joan became highly defensive blaming the failure on the firm. She accused the company of not providing sufficient advertising and other support activities. She resisted any intervention on the part of Harriet Johnson, the firm's sales manager, arguing that she would run "her" office as she saw fit.

Harriet, who has been sales manager for less than a year has backed off, not wanting to risk losing Joan. The firm is expanding the advertising budget for the office hoping the situation improves. The two broker/owners suggest ideas they think might help Joan at the weekly managers' meetings, although they avoid directing them at her because of her sensitivity.

Guidelines for a Solution As in the preceeding case, we can see the failure of the sales manager to deal decisively with the situation. The longer the situation persists, the more difficult Joan's attitude problem is going to become. It is likely that not only will the office fail, but the firm will lose Joan, an accomplished producer, as well.

Once again, the sales manager must take direct action, engaging Joan in a one-on-one conversation on the problems facing the branch. Harriet hasn't done this for the same reason Karen avoided dealing with many of the office managers who kept going to Frank. She doesn't know how to address the conflict effectively. Harriet fears the discussion will result in an argument which will make the situation worse instead of better.

This, in fact, emerged from interviews as the principal reason for procrastination in dealing with these kinds of problems. Giving constructive criticism is one of the most difficult managerial functions that confront a broker.

Several lessons can be learned from each of the above cases. First, procrastination usually makes the situation more difficult to resolve. Attitudes harden, ineffective behavior settles into a pattern, and constructively addressing the situation becomes increasingly difficult. Further, confronting the problem in a direct, person-to-person fashion (a 9,9 approach) is frequently the only adequate method of resolving the problem. Oblique references, hints or other roundabout methods of dealing with the problem almost never work. One common reason for a broker to procrastinate in dealing with a problem such as we have been discussing is lack of confidence in how to successfully address the issue. *The fear is that confronting the problem will lead to a confrontation with the person.* From experience, the broker knows that if that happens, the doors leading to successful resolution of the problem rapidly close.

How to Manage Conflict Situations

Our discussion deals with the question of how to confront a problem directly without creating an adversary relationship with the other person. In other words, what is the practical approach of the 9,9 manager?

Success in managing interpersonal conflict rests on a fundamental principle of behavior: *people's actions are based on their own perceptions.* In order to get someone to change his mind, his opinion or behavior, that person must come to perceive things differently. This is hardly news to successful salespeople. Yet, for some reason it often gets forgotten when a successful salesperson moves into management.

We also know from experience that facts alone seldom change the perceptions of others. What is needed is not additional information, but a change in perspective. To change the perspective of another person requires that we provide an opportunity for them to alter their feelings or sentiments about an issue so they view the facts of the situation differently. So we return to the distinction made in Chapter 1 between fact and sentiment.

Exhibit 4

When Managing Conflict

Facts x o = o
Facts x Feeling = Commitment

What are the feelings which Karen and Harriet can expect to encounter? In Karen's case, there are a range of possible feelings which the branch managers and sales associates may be experiencing:

1. Insecurity about the new situation, based on the loss of a close and comfortable relationship with Frank.
2. Loss of the "family" feeling in the firm.
3. Resentment over Karen because she and not they got the promotion.
4. Questions about Karen's ability to perform the job.

Harriet, on the other hand, can expect to deal with an equally, if not more volatile, set of feelings on the part of Joan:

1. A sense of failure.
2. Loss of face with her peers.
3. Disappointment with the firm's approach to the new office.
4. Insecurity over what happens next.

When Karen and Harriet attempt to deal with their respective subordinates, their most difficult problem will be remembering that it makes little difference whether or not there is any logical basis for these feelings. These are issues of sentiment and are of an non-logical nature. If either Karen or Harriet attempts to refute these feelings with facts they will meet with increased resistance from the other person. Imagine the following dialogue:

Branch Manager: Let's be honest about it, the strength of this firm has always been the family feeling Frank generated. Now, we can't deal with him.

Karen: But with the firm getting as large as it is, Frank couldn't continue to have enough contact with everyone to maintain that feeling anyway.

Branch Manager: But, still, we were able to talk with him; now we don't know what he is thinking.

Karen: However, I talk with Frank every day and can respond to any questions you have. Besides, Frank wants me to resolve operating problems. He's depending on us to work as a team, and with a little effort we can. Anyway, you'll still see Frank at meetings.

Branch Manager: But, it's more awkward now. And my people only see him when he happens to stop in the office.

What's happening here? Karen and the manager are locked in adversary postures. Little progress is being made to resolve the problem. Karen may eventually wear down the manager, but she won't convince him. Karen is responding to the manager by saying "Yes, but." Of course, sometimes she implies the "but" rather than actually saying it, but it is still there. Feelings, it turns out, are remarkably resistant to "yes, but" responses.

The truth of the matter is that adversary discussions seldom resolve conflict. Even though they appear to work at times, with the subordinate party giving in, debris is usually left behind in the form of smoldering resentment, hurt feelings, damaged egos, and a strong desire by the loser to "get even." In situations where continuity of a cooperative relationship is essential, use of an adversary approach can be very destructive. Consequently, another approach is needed.

The basic objective of the conflict management model described below is to integrate as much as possible the needs, interests and objectives of both parties into the discussion. This is the heart of the 9,9 approach. When attempting to influence others, a broker is most successful when the other people are able to see for themselves the merits in the broker's position. The key to success is satisfying the other person's needs. This requires being able to answer the two fundamental questions which are on the other person's mind: "How will this affect me?" and "How will I benefit?" To achieve this objective, the broker must attempt to understand the attitudes, feelings and opinions of the sales associate.

The five–step model described below summarizes the key skills necessary for resolving conflict.

A Model for Managing Conflict

Step 1: State the Purpose—The Problem—Your Proposal

When raising a delicate or sensitive issue with another person, it is best to *be direct*. Beating around the bush, making small talk, hinting or other methods of getting at the issue are seldom effective. Confusion and uncertainty are the usual by-products of such approaches. Clarity is an important, and all too often neglected, dimension of effective communication.

Exhibit 5
A Model for Managing Conflict

Step 1:	State the purpose - the problem - your proposal
Step 2:	Explore the differences
Step 3:	Sharpen the differences
Step 4:	Develop alternatives
Step 5:	Obtain agreement

When directing criticism toward another person it is essential to get to the point. Sometimes a broker will begin the conversation by asking a broad question like, "How are things going?" or "How do you feel about your development to date with the firm?" If the broker is simply interested in learning about the sales associate's feelings about his situation, with no specific problem in mind, then there is nothing wrong with such an opening. However, assuming the broker already knows the answer, such an opening is likely to come across as phony and an attempt to set up the salesperson. For example:

Broker:	How do you think things have been going?
Sales Associate:	Hectic as usual. I've been working hard this month.
Broker:	How is your sales volume?
Sales Associate:	All right. I think things are picking up.
Broker:	Well, I think you're being a little overly optimistic. I was reviewing your numbers recently and ...

Sounds terrible, doesn't it? The broker knew all along he wanted to talk to the sales associate about his recent performance, so why didn't he come right to the point? How much better it would have been for him to have said, "Frank, in reviewing your numbers I've noticed your sales are down 20 percent from last year. Let's talk about the situation." Now the issue is on the table and the broker and the sales associate can focus on it.

Notice that the above opening is *descriptive,* not evaluative. As we learned in Chapter 2, descriptive comments elicit less defensiveness from the other person while directing his or her attention toward the specific issue the broker wishes to discuss. When approaching a member of the firm about a problem which is likely to be met by resistance on his part, always describe the situation. Do not attack the person.

For example, in our first case in this chapter, Karen should open a discussion with one of the branch managers who has been going directly to Frank by saying something like, "Ed, yesterday you called Frank to ask about whether we would accept a rental property in another town. Later I found out about the decision from one of your salespeople. I would like to talk about that." In our second case, Harriet will have to approach Joan directly by stating, "We have been getting 60 percent fewer listings in Franklin then we had hoped for. This has kept the office in a loss situation for more than six months. I want to discuss the situation with you and come up with some ideas for improvement."

Being descriptive, it should be noted, holds for discussions with non-sales as well as sales personnel. If you have any questions on descriptive statements, review Chapter 2 carefully.

Whenever you are approaching a member of the firm with a proposal which involves their participation, be sure to tell him why you believe the change is necessary and how he will benefit. Because the other person may not even understand why you are bringing up the matter it may be necessary to briefly summarize the problem or event which prompted your investigation and your resulting proposal.

Avoid making the presentation long and involved. In most cases, it is better to err on the side of brevity. Most salespeople don't like long-winded presentations. Besides, a short, concise presentation enables the other person to get involved early in the discussion by asking for additional data or by voicing his or her reaction. In this way, the broker knows that the other person is *listening*. It gives the broker a better clue to the sales associate's needs and interests at that moment. If the presentation is too long, the other person may actually resist early in the presentation, stop listening, and spend the remaining time developing a rebuttal.

Step 2: Explore the Differences

Once the proposal or problem is on the table, the broker's attention needs to be directed toward the other person's reaction. If the other person is in agreement, then the conversation can focus on the next steps which are to be taken. However, the other person will frequently have questions, reservations or excuses. It is to the broker's advantage to explore these reactions in depth.

This is the critical point in the discussion, the place where the adversary posture is most likely to emerge. If, when the other person voices an objection, the broker says "Yes, but" the first step toward the adversary posture has been taken.

Avoiding an adversary response is as difficult as it is preferable. After all, the broker feels strongly about the issue too. And he has probably given the matter a lot of thought. When he encounters resistance from the other person, the broker often feels the need to defend his position. This is natural. However, if the broker succumbs to it, the conversation is likely to deteriorate into a battle of two defensive systems. Yes, it takes a strong, self-confident ego to avoid an adversary posture.

Actually, it is foolish for the broker to expect the other person to accept his description of the situation at face value. As we learned in Chapter 1, people rarely perceive the same event in identical terms. The broker should anticipate the other person having a different perspective on the issue.

Further, if the problem involves the other person's performance, it is to be expected that a person with strong achievement needs will attempt to defend himself. After all, even average sales producers are used to influencing others, not to being influenced.

Seen in this light, the problem in the case of the failing office manager is not so much Harriet's defensiveness, as her immediate manager's inability to deal with it.

There is another, data-based, reason for avoiding arguing with the objection. *Studies show that in conflict situations, the first objection or excuse is the real one only 2 to 24 percent of the time.* Think about that piece of data. What it means is that if the broker gets into an argument with the other person's early objections, not only is he into an adversary relationship, but usually over the wrong thing!

There are several reasons why a person doesn't share his or her real thinking during the early stages of a conversation. Among the more common are:

1. The person is protecting the real reason. As a subordinate once said to me, "If I don't tell you what's bothering me, you can't win!"
2. The person is embarrassed by the real reason or otherwise finds it difficult to talk about.
3. The person isn't sure of his real reaction himself, so he says the first thing that comes to mind.

Apply the Listening Skills The lesson should be obvious. Once the problem has been stated, the broker's immediate objective is to learn as much as possible about the other person's reaction. To get this underway the broker merely has to ask a simple question, "What do you think of my proposal?" However, as we have just seen, to gain a full understanding of the attitudes, feelings and opinions of the other person, the broker must do more than merely accept the other person's first response. The broker must continue to draw out the other person. The managerial tools for doing this are the listening skills learned in Chapter 2:

- Open-ended questions
- Directed or linking questions
- Expanders
- Restatement and reflection
- Silence

The broker should be using the above tools to actively explore the area of disagreement. The more the broker does this, the more likely it is the area of disagreement will come to seem smaller than it appeared at first.

Have you ever been in a conversation with a friend, spouse or colleague and about 15 minutes into the discussion found one of you saying something like "I think it is all a matter of semantics" or "I don't think we really disagree that much?" Ever wonder why this happens? The reason is that as we talk, we tend to change our mind somewhat as the real issues become clearer to us. Getting the other person talking, without challenging him with adversary responses, gives him a chance to talk through proposals or problems and perhaps change his perceptions.

This is especially important when the other person is expressing a strongly felt position. Only by giving him a chance to get his feelings off his chest can we hope to make progress. Many times, once someone has an opportunity to express his feelings, they will be more open to facts.

A parallel situation exists when the broker is critically discussing a sales associate's job performance. Criticizing someone is like throwing a rock at their ego. An excuse on his part is like building a fence to protect himself from the rocks. When we tear the fence down (attack the excuse) the other person usually builds another. As long as his energies are being channeled into building fences it is unlikely he will closely examine the situation we are describing.

By neither agreeing nor disagreeing with the excuse, but using our listening skills to invite the person to elaborate on the excuse, we are letting the person have his fence. We can then move the conversation along by asking what other things might be contributing to the problem. Hopefully, he will then be more willing to peer over the fence and talk with us.

There is another important benefit of exploring the differences with the other person: the broker gets information on the other person's problems. In short, the flow of information is from the other person to the broker. Such a flow is necessary if the broker is to have a chance at resolving the situation to the benefit of all parties concerned.

In sum, by using the listening skills to probe and understand the person's reaction the broker

1. creates a climate in which the other person can talk through the broker's position, clarifying the issues involved and often changing his mind in the process.
2. diffuses the other person's defensiveness (while avoiding a defensive reaction on the part of the broker).
3. generates information necessary to understanding the other person's point of view and the problems he faces.

Step 3: Sharpen the Differences

By continuing to explore the differences until he understands the other person's feelings on the issue, the broker will usually uncover a number of areas of agreement and disagreement. The next step is to sharpen the real differences between the broker and the other person. Let's see how this can be done.

A question which often arises is "How do I know when I have got down to the real objections?" This requires judgment. Watch and listen for clues. Here are a few:

1. Sometimes the other person will state, "What it really comes down to is this. . . ."
2. Sometimes the conversation keeps returning to one or two key points.
3. Sometimes it is evident from non-verbal signals that the person feels more strongly about certain issues than others.
4. Sometimes it becomes obvious the person is attempting to avoid mentioning some aspect of the problem. Here the broker has to descriptively introduce the topic himself and carefully read the other person's reaction.

When the broker feels he understands the other person's position, he should test his understanding by sharpening the differences. An easy way to do this is to summarize your understanding of the other person's perceptions of the whole situation. The broker might say, for example, "Let's see where we stand. As I understand it, we agree on points A, B, C and D but you feel that points E and F are a poor approach. Is that right?" When the differences are focused on in this way, one of two things will happen. The other person will say, "Yes, I think that is right," in which case the broker can move on and begin to discuss solutions. At this point the broker has the sales associate's acknowledgement that he understands the problem, a good starting point for agreement.

Or the sales associate will say, "No, that's not exactly right; there are some other problems here. . .", which is a signal to the broker that he must back up and further explore the other person's feelings. When the broker feels he has an understanding of the sales associate's point of view, he can again test and sharpen the differences.

Let's take time here to analyze the importance of Step 3. This step accomplishes a couple of things. First, it begins to build a bridge between the broker and the sales associate. Basic agreement is built upon those areas where two parties share common interests, ideas, beliefs or needs. By summarizing the areas of common agreement, the broker helps to get the bridgework of understanding under way. For example, in the second case discussed at the beginning of this chapter, if Harriet can get Joan to agree that both want to see the office at maximum possible production, then at least one common denominator of mutual self-interest has been found. And this has been accomplished without glossing over the areas of disagreement. Ignoring areas of disagreement often leaves subordinates feeling their problems have been whitewashed, a feeling which is not likely to result in a positive attitude toward the firm. At the conclusion of Step 3, the broker has the sales associate's agreement that she understands the reasons for disagreement, which is a strong support in the bridgework we have been building.

A second but equally important result of Step 3 is that it provides a natural springboard into the solution-finding step. If Step 2 has been thoroughly utilized, the conversation has probably covered a range of issues. Step 3 pulls the discussion together, making it possible to *focus* a solution on the areas of true disagreement. Once the sales associate agrees, it is easy for the broker to say, "Well, since we now know where we agree and disagree, let's see what we can do to get together on this thing."

Thus, while Step 3 is a brief step it is an important one. In the eagerness of wanting to arrive at a resolution of the conflict it is easy to forget about the importance of this step. In fact, being so eager to arrive at solutions that Step 2 is short–circuited and Step 3 is ignored is a common mistake.

Step 4: Develop Alternatives

Having identified aspects of the situation where there is agreement and areas where some differences still exist, the broker can then explore alternative solutions with the sales associate. The broker can ask the sales associate for suggestions as well as proposing ideas of his own. Each alternative should be directed toward the specific remaining areas of disagreement.

The key to using alternatives effectively is to compare the alternatives one against each other. If an original proposal is involved compare the alternatives against the original idea. The listening skills can be used to encourage discussion. Now is the time to introduce facts into the conversation in the form of pro and con arguments relative to the options available.

It is critical that the broker help the sales associate examine the positive and negative aspects of each alternative. This can easily be accomplished by saying something like, "Let's see, if we were to try this it seems to me we gain some things and we lose some things. What we gain is ..."

Remember, no solution is likely to be all good or all bad. Almost every idea has advantages and disadvantages. Unfortunately, we tend to focus on the disadvantages of someone else's ideas. Begin observing what happens when someone makes a suggestion. Nine out of ten times what happens? Right! The listener starts talking about what's wrong with the idea. The effect of this is to reduce the number of helpful ideas offered during a conversation and to increase defensiveness and conflict.

An effective antidote to this problem is to offer positive comments *first* when someone makes a suggestion and *then* to identify those facets of the suggestion that are negative. George Prince refers to this practice as employing the "spectrum policy."[3] Prince observes that almost all ideas have *both* good and bad features (i.e., a spectrum of qualities) but that by pouncing first on the bad features we never even *get* to the good ones. Prince further observes that this often leads us to cast out the *entire* idea, thus not retaining even the good parts.

The lesson of Prince's spectrum policy for Step 4 of the model is both direct and valuable. When the sales associate offers alternatives, first focus on the possible advantages of the idea. Then examine the possible downsides which need to be taken into consideration. This will often lead to the building of composite ideas, as suggestions are dissected into good and bad parts.

The main point is to give the other person an opportunity to weigh the alternatives, coming to an understanding of the courses of action open to him. When this happens something critical occurs to the other person's choice space. As long as only one course of action is available, the other person has the choice of agreeing or disagreeing. However, when alternatives are considered simultaneously, there is more than one agreement possibility. The practical effect of this is that disagreeing is no longer half the other person's decision space. Smart managers recognize this and use it in the conflict management process. Exhibit 6 illustrates this principle.

All the alternatives should be ones the broker can live with. If a given alternative does not seem feasible, the broker should say so. Then explore the other options. But flexibility is the key to the conflict resolution process.

If the conflict involves a performance problem, certain critical variables need to be considered during the solution–finding process. These are thoroughly presented in Chapter 4. However, the general principles outlined above still hold.

Exhibit 6
Impact of Options On the Other Person's Choice Space

With one solution available

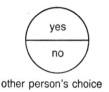

other person's choice

With two options on the table

other person's choice

With three options on the table

other person's choice

Step 5: Obtain Agreement

Having enabled the other person to express his or her views without being attacked and having given that person the opportunity to thoroughly examine the situation from various angles, the broker is in a position of working with, and not against, the sales associate. The broker can now move toward a solution acceptable to both parties. Often the sales associate will select the most feasible alternative.

Summary

The above model represents an approach for dealing with conflict situations. Using the model effectively requires practice, but experience has demonstrated that this basic approach can help a broker or sales manager keep open lines of communication during difficult situations. The reader will notice that the model draws on the core skills learned in Chapter 2 as well as requiring some additional communication techniques. Exhibit 7 summarizes the model along with the skills.

Exercise 3-B can help you test your understanding of the model.

Exhibit 7
Summary of the Steps and Skills of
Conflict Management

Step 1: *State the purpose - the problem - your proposal*

Key skills - be direct
be brief
be descriptive

Step 2: *Explore the differences*

Key skills - questions - open-ended and directed
expanders
restatement
reflection
silence

Step 3: *Sharpen the differences*

Key skills - summarizing the areas of agreement
and disagreement

Step 4: *Development alternatives*

Key skills - comparing alternatives
spectrum policy

Step 5: *Obtain agreement*

Exercise 3-A
Management Style Analysis*

Instructions: For each of the statements (1, 2, 3, 4, and 5) select the alternative which is most characteristic of your attitudes or actions and place a [1] by that alternative, then place a [2] by the attitude or action which is second most characteristic of you and so on until you have ranked all five alternatives *under each statement.* Indicate your answers on these pages in the space provided. For the most accurate self-diagnosis, answer in terms of what you *actually* think or do — *not* what you believe to be the "correct" answer.

Below are some questions which are designed to help you think about your management style, especially as it relates to managing conflict.

1. As a manager, my major responsibility is to achieve firm goals by
   _____ A getting them accomplished — regardless of how.
   _____ B seeing to it that harmonious, cooperative relationships between people are established and maintained.
   _____ C carrying out established and proven procedures.
   _____ D by finding a balance so a reasonable degree of production can be achieved without destroying morale.
   _____ E getting more people to contribute their ideas.

2. In making decisions on work related problems, I mainly
   _____ A refer problems to others for decisions.
   _____ B try to encourage decisions which are the result of debate and deliberation by those who have relevant knowledge.
   _____ C rely heavily on my own skills, knowledge, and past experience.
   _____ D look for decisions which to a large extent reflect the ideas and opinions the majority will support.
   _____ E get a reading on how others think, then make the final decisions myself.

3. When I find myself in conflict with my sales staff, I usually
   _____ A take a stand and try to get my points across.
   _____ B am quiet — not outspoken.
   _____ C try to find out what the others think before I express myself.

---

*©Copyright by Drake-Beam & Associates. Used by permission.

_____D   try to work for a reasonable compromise.

_____E   communicate my feelings and the information I have available.

4. When I find myself in conflict with my staff, I usually

_____A   allow a cooling off period until a blending of different positions is possible.

_____B   try to smooth over the trouble and do something to release tension that has built up.

_____C   try not to get involved further by stirring up the issue.

_____D   use my authority to halt the conflict.

_____E   bring the individuals together and meet the issues directly.

5. As far as creativity is concerned, I go on the assumption that innovation

_____A   is most encouraged by a manager who uncritically accepts ideas his people present.

_____B   is most encouraged by a manager who creates competition among his employees by the use of rewards.

_____C   is most encouraged by a manager who creates conditions wherein "brainstorming" or other such devices can be used.

_____D   is most encouraged by a manager who allows experimentation.

_____E   is something no manager can encourage or hinder by his actions; it is unrelated to the condition of any specific work situation.

Exercise 3-A
Analysis Answer Sheet

Instructions: Place your answers in the appropriate space below.
For example: if you answered 1.C with a 2, place the 2 beside 1.C.

9.9	5.5	9.1	1.9	1.1
1.E_____	1.D_____	1.A_____	1.B_____	1.C_____
2.B_____	2.E_____	2.C_____	2.D_____	2.A_____
3.E_____	3.D_____	3.A_____	3.C_____	3.B_____
4.E_____	4.A_____	4.D_____	4.B_____	4.C_____
5.D_____	5.C_____	5.B_____	5.A_____	5.E_____

Totals:_____   _____   _____   _____   _____

Your lowest score indicates your preferred management style as you
described yourself on the questionnaire. Your next lowest score is
your backup style. The wider the spread between the two the more
likely you are to use your preferred style over your backup. A tie
represents a blend of the styles.

Exercise 3-B
Conflict Management Questionnaire—A Check on Views

Below are several questions about conflict management situations. Each question is followed by several possible answers. Please select the answer which comes closest to what you think is the most effective way to handle the situation that is described, according to the conflict management model learned in Chapter 3. Indicate your answer with a checkmark in the space before the option you think is correct. Assume all situations refer to people in the firm—these are management situations.

1. Once I have outlined my recommendation to another person, I
    _____ask the person if he or she has any questions about it.
    _____ask the person for his or her reaction to my idea.
    _____sum up the key advantages of my idea.

2. When a sales manager says, "Your point is well taken, but I can't change right now," I react to it in the same manner as I would if the person said,
    _____"No."
    _____"No, and I don't want to talk about it now."
    _____"Yes, let's discuss it again at a later time."

3. When I encounter a strong objection to my argument, I try to
    _____offset the objection by re-emphasizing, in a slightly different way, the positive value of the idea.
    _____move on to another point that has a better chance of acceptance.
    _____see why the objection was raised.

4. A sales associate reacted favorably to my recommendation, but raised a serious objection. We discussed this point, and the associate seemed to agree the objection had been answered. My next move is to
    _____indicate to the associate, "I'll move ahead with it."
    _____ask if the associate has other objections.
    _____restate the benefits of my idea with special emphasis on the point I had just made.
    _____remain silent to see what other objections may be raised.

5. At times, people accept part of a recommendation, but reject a

portion of it despite my efforts to reach agreement. In these cases, I

_____push a little harder than usual for acceptance of the entire idea since I already have achieved some agreement.

_____take the accepted part now and try to "sell" the rest later.

_____come back later with the same idea, but begin anew; the idea being that a "different day and different mood" may be more appropriate.

_____come back later with the same idea, but with a few minor revisions.

_____come back with an extensively revised recommendation since total acceptance is highly unlikely.

6. I complete the presentation of a recommendation and my sales associate does not react positively or negatively. The best action is

_____restate the features and benefits of the idea.

_____ask for questions or comments

_____ask if my associate would like to think over the proposal.

_____keep silent and wait for my associate's reaction.

_____assume my sales associate has accepted my idea and ask a question which must be answered with acceptance or rejection.

7. In developing my abilities to manage conflict, I concentrate primarily on improving my

_____ability to communicate with others.

_____professional skill or competence.

_____ability to identify the needs of others.

_____ability to develop sound proposals.

8. I try to gain acceptance of my ideas by relying heavily upon

_____the facts of my proposal.

_____relating my proposal to the perceived needs of the person I am trying to influence.

_____a forceful, aggressive approach.

_____clear, objective answers to potential objections that others may raise.

See Scoring Guide on p.64. For each answer, give yourself the number of points indicated.

Exercise 3-B
Scoring Guide—Conflict Management
Questionnaire

Number of Points
32 or more = excellent
24 to 32 = very good
16 to 24 = fair (some conflict)
16 or less = wow!

1. Once I have outlined my recommendation to another person, I
   __3__ask the person if he or she has any questions about it.
   __5__ask the person for his or her reaction to my idea.
   __0__sum up the key advantages of my idea.

2. When a sales manager says, "Your point is well taken, but I can't change right now," I react to it in the same manner as I would if the person said,
   __5__"No."
   __3__"No, and I don't want to talk about it now."
   __0__"Yes, let's discuss it again at a later time."

3. When I encounter a strong objection to my argument, I try to
   __0__offset the objection by re-emphasizing, in a slightly different way, the positive value of the idea.
   __2__move on to another point that has a better chance of acceptance.
   __5__see why the objection was raised.

4. A sales associate reacted favorably to my recommendation, but raised a serious objection. We discussed this point, and the associate seemed to agree the objection had been answered. My next move is to
   __4__indicate to the associate, "I'll move ahead with it,"
   __5__ask if the associate has other objections.
   __0__restate the benefits of my idea with special emphasis on the point I just made.
   __3__remain silent to see what other objections may be raised.

5. At times, people accept part of a recommendation, but reject a portion of it despite my efforts to reach agreement. In these cases, I

___0___push a little harder than usual for acceptance of the entire idea since I already have achieved some agreement.

___5___take the accepted part now, and try to "sell" the rest later.

___3___come back later with the same idea, but begin anew; the idea being that a "different day and different mood" may be more appropriate.

___2___come back later with the same idea, but with a few minor revisions.

___1___come back with an extensively revised recommendation since total acceptance is highly unlikely.

6. I complete the presentation of a recommendation and my sales associate does not react positively or negatively. The best action is

___0___restate the features and benefits of the idea.

___5___ask for questions or comments.

___0___ask if my associate would like to think over the proposal.

___2___keep silent and wait for my associate's reaction.

___3___assume my associate has accepted my idea and ask a question which must be answered with acceptance or rejection.

7. In developing my abilities to manage conflict, I concentrate primarily on improving my

___4___ability to communicate with others.

___4___professional skill or competence.

___5___ability to identify the needs of others.

___3___ability to develop sound proposals.

8. I try to gain acceptance of my ideas by relying heavily upon:

___0___the facts of my proposal.

___5___relating my proposal to the perceived needs of the person I am trying to influence.

___0___ a forceful, aggressive approach.

___3___clear, objective answers to potential objections that others may raise.

Footnotes for Chapter 3

1. See *Real Estate Office Management, People, Functions, Systems* (Chicago: REALTORS NATIONAL MARKETING INSTITUTE®, 1975). Chapter 16.

2. *The Managerial Grid* ® figure from *The New Managerial Grid*, by Robert R. Blake and Jane Srygley Mouton. Houston: Gulf Publishing Company, 1978, p.11. Reproduced by permission.

3. George M. Prince, *The Practice of Creativity* (New York: Collier Books, 1970).

Chapter 4

Problem-Solving: The Art of Giving Constructive Criticism

Without question, criticizing others is one of the most difficult managerial tasks. Most new managers find it an unpleasant exercise and individuals who are good at it usually enjoy the admiration of their peers. Who hasn't heard the compliment, given in grudging respect, "He can rip you apart and have you leave the office thanking him."

Such responses need not be restricted to the "natural" communicator, the manager whose style is uniquely his own. Successfully giving constructive criticism is a learnable managerial skill.

Criticizing others is a form of conflict management. The sales manager whose office is not performing up to expectations, the sales associate whose approach to getting listings is less than effective, and the secretary who handles potential buyers poorly are all candidates for criticism. And in all probability each will go on the defensive when criticized.

Effective Criticism Requires Problem Solving

The managerial intent of criticism is improved performance. Criticism without subsequent improvement is of little business value. Experience teaches us that improvement in performance is dependent on the problem solving skills of the broker.

If sales associates believe the broker's criticism is motivated by a desire to surface and resolve problems, then subsequent motivation to improve is likely to be high. As with any conflict situation, the key to translating criticism into improved performance lies in obtaining agreement from the other person that a problem exists.

Progress toward eliciting this agreement can be facilitated by following the first two steps of the conflict management model learned in Chapter 3. Performance criticism should be stated in the same fashion as any problem which is likely to generate conflict—*descriptively*. Yet no matter how descriptively the broker may describe the problem, the sales associate is likely to defend himself with excuses. If the broker attempts to minimize these excuses or knock them down, an adversary relationship is established. Use of listening skills to encourage the sales associate to discuss the issue will serve to both lower his defensiveness and provide information on how he perceives the problem.

When dealing with performance problems, the broker utilizes the listening steps to identify and get agreement on the real problem—the cause of the behavior which the broker is criticizing. As we shall see, identifying the real problem is germane to improvement. Depending on the real source of the criticized behavior, the kind of solution which is appropriate will vary.

Three Steps to Identifying and Agreeing on the Problem

The first step is getting the sales associate to agree that the situation which is being described has occurred. For example, if the broker has observed that the sales associate has a tendency to interrupt others, the first order of business is to get agreement that this happens. Sometimes this will require several descriptive illustrations to elicit agreement from the other person. Other times agreement will be fairly straightforward.

Once agreement on the situation is reached, the broker can use his listening skills to identify the symptoms associated with it. Symptoms are the behaviors which contribute to the situation. For example, has the sales associate been aware of his tendency to interrupt others? Under what conditions is he most likely to do so? By exploring symptoms we often get a clue to the real source of the situation—*the problem*. Consider the following dialogue:

Broker:	Alice, I have noticed that when you deal with potential buyers you frequently interrupt them in mid-sentence. I think this results in your not always getting a complete understanding of the sales possibilities.
Alice:	Oh, I don't think so. I'm just a good conversationalist.
Broker:	Well, the reason why I brought it up is that in talking with the Johnsons I learned that they were more open to a ranch style home than I think you understood them to be. A similar thing occurred with the Franklins earlier this month. In thinking about why, I observed this tendency ... (*shortly into the conversation*)
Alice:	I guess sometimes I am a little eager to talk. This is the first I've thought about it, really.
Broker:	What do you suppose causes that?
Alice:	(*thinking*) I don't know ... just enthusiasm, I guess. When I think I have something the buyer might like, I get pretty enthusiastic.
Broker:	How do you approach the buyer?
Alice:	As much as possible I try to size up what his needs are.
Broker:	Do you think in your enthusiasm you sometimes jump to conclusions?
Alice:	(*pause*) I suppose I do, now that you mention it. A friend of mine commented on this same thing. She said I always finish her sentences for her.
Broker:	Where do you think that habit comes from?
Alice:	I've always been that way. It's just me, I guess.
Broker:	We seem to be saying that at times your

	enthusiasm tends to lead you to jump to conclusions and as a result, you sometimes stop listening to a potential buyer. This is just part of how you are. Is that right?
Alice:	Yes, I think so.
Broker:	I would agree with that. I think your enthusiasm is one of your strengths. It's just that here we see an instance where it can sometimes get in the way of understanding the real needs of the buyer. Let's see if there isn't some way you can avoid this particular problem ....

If we analyze this conversation we see that the broker concisely and descriptively got to the purpose of the discussion. And he continued to discuss it in a descriptive fashion. Once he got agreement on the situation—i.e., that Alice tends to interrupt people—he used his listening skills to explore the symptoms which might be part of this tendency. This led to Alice's realizing that she tends to jump to conclusions. Notice how the broker used a close-ended question to get her to focus on this particular possibility.

Finally they agreed on the problem—this is part of Alice's personality (we will learn more about types of problems in just a little bit). At this point the broker sharpened the area of agreement so that he was in a position to direct the conversation toward a solution. This is a variation of Step 3 of our conflict management model.

This process is illustrated by Exhibit 8.

REALTORS® will often confuse symptoms and problems. Consider the receptionist-secretary who has a tendency to forget to follow through on certain instructions and is frequently behind in her typing. In talking with her the broker finds her approach to her work is disorganized. Often the broker will say, "She's too disorganized," thinking that disorganization is the problem. However, the real problem is whatever is causing her to be disorganized. For example, perhaps she is disorganized because the broker is disorganized and is always changing her work priorities. Here the problem is the broker. Or maybe she doesn't know how to organize her work. Or possibly it is just her personality to be disroganized. The solution to the problem will be different, depending on which of these is the *real* source of her disorganization.

Let's examine the issue of identifying the problem more closely.

Exhibit 8
Key Steps In The Problem Solving Process

The broker presents the problem in a descriptive fashion . . . .

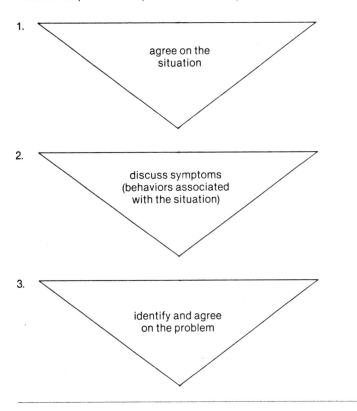

1. agree on the situation

2. discuss symptoms (behaviors associated with the situation)

3. identify and agree on the problem

Some Possible Problems

When attempting to help a staff member improve his or her performance, it is helpful if the broker has a set of possible problems which can be used to organize his thinking. Below is a list of potential problems which experience indicates is helpful in thinking about most performance difficulties. Perhaps not every poor performance situation can be classified as falling into one or some combination of these problem categories, but most will.

Others—Outside Influences

The problem may not lie directly with the sales associate but may be created by other people or outside influences. For example:

- A spouse who is placing pressure on the sales associate for working long or late hours.
- The broker himself. Perhaps his style of operation is highly disorganized, creating confusion or chaos. Or the broker could be undermining the manager's authority by dealing with salespeople himself.
- A personal problem at home.
- Some bad personal investments which require a disproportionate amount of the sales associate's time.

Knowledge and Experience

The problem is knowledge and experience when the sales associate is not performing well because he was never taught the proper methods necessary for success.

Firms where the broker takes a "sink or swim" attitude toward performance are often characterized by exceptionally high failure rates as new sales associates attempt to compete against the well-trained staffs of other firms.

Motivation

The sales associate simply lacks the motivation to perform.

If he is honest with himself he just doesn't like certain aspects of the job and avoids them. For example, he doesn't like paperwork and therefore fails to keep adequate records of leads and prior sales.

Personality

The sales associate has some trait or quality which creates difficulties for himself.

For instance, he is impatient or overly aggressive or stubborn in his approach to others.

Aptitude

The sales associate has poor aptitude or capacity for sales work.

For example, a salesperson may lack the verbal aptitude to be successful. Aptitude is the problem when all the other possible problem areas have been eliminated, e.g., the sales associate has received adequate training, is clearly working hard, has no obvious personality traits which are blocking his success and no other influences seem to be present.

In probing and exploring the symptoms, the broker should attempt to determine which of the above problems is at the root of the difficulty. For example, in discussing a problem which involves a sales associate who has a tendency to interrupt others during conversations, the broker needs to explore why this happens. Consider the following dialogue:

Broker:	(*getting agreement on the situation*) So you can see that you have this tendency to cut people short?
Sales Associate:	Now that we are discussing it, yes. I guess it can turn some people off.
Broker:	Well, let's see if we can't understand what happens a little better. Then maybe you can guard against it. What do you think causes it?
Sales Associate:	Well I never really thought about it before, although I guess my husband has kidded me about being so talkative.
Broker:	(*restating*) You always have been talkative.
Sales Associate:	Yes, I guess so. It's just me. You know when I get excited I want to tell the buyer as much as possible. I guess I lose sight of their reactions.
Broker:	(*restating*) That's just the way you are.
Sales Associate:	Yes.

In the above dialogue, the broker and the sales associate seem to agree that the problem is "just the way she is;" in other words, a personality problem. Of course the sales associate doesn't have to admit "I have a personality problem" or "I have a motivation problem." But if the broker and the sales associate can agree that he has certain "personal characteristics" which at times tend to block his sales effectiveness, or the associate just "doesn't like to do certain things and therefore avoids them," the same thing has been accomplished. The astute broker will understand the true nature of the problem and can proceed accordingly.

Involving the Sales Associate in Finding Solutions

Once the sales associate has accepted that he has a problem, the broker can move toward gaining his participation in working out practical solutions to the problem. The importance of involving the subordinate in the solution-finding process is a matter of practicality and commitment.

Involving the sales associate in answering the question "What can we do about the problem?" is practical because he is likely to select some solution which has a reasonable chance of being achieved. To the extent that the proposed solution is his idea, stated in his terms, a much greater degree of motivation is likely than if the broker had evolved the plan on his own.

This can be accomplished quite readily once the problem has been identified. Returning to our general conflict management model, the broker can sharpen the issues by summarizing the conversation. "Let's see, we seem to be saying that your tendency to interrupt seems to come out of your enthusiasm for the job. When you are enthusiastic you sometimes get so caught up in what you are saying that you lose sight of the other person's wishes? Is that right?" When the sales associate agrees, the broker can move into the solution-finding step by stating, "If that's the case and you can see how that is hurting you, we probably should see what you might do to minimize the problem." "What thoughts do you have on how you might go about working on this trait?"

This is not to imply that the broker cannot play an active role during the solution finding stage. In all probability the sales associate will look to the broker for guidance in thinking about how to improve. The broker should offer his thoughts and ideas and discuss them jointly with the sales associate. Further, the astute broker, knowing the nature of the problem, will be able to sort through the *kinds of corrective actions which fit the problem.*

Matching Solutions to Problems

The details of the solution will, of course, be individualized to the person involved. However, one important value of identifying the real problem is that it suggests *what kind of solution is appropriate.* Experience demonstrates that certain types of solutions clearly match up to each of the five possible problems we discussed above. The broker is thus in a position to guide the sales associate toward a workable solution.

Exhibit 9 illustrates the relationship between problems and solutions. More specifically, consider the following examples.

Others/Outside Influences
Experience indicates that there is a range of possible solutions, some of which the broker can at least partially control.

Solution 1: Broker Changes His Behavior Sometimes the most difficult thing in management is to recognize when we (management) are the problem. For example, one broker, after much soul

Exhibit 9
Problems and Solutions

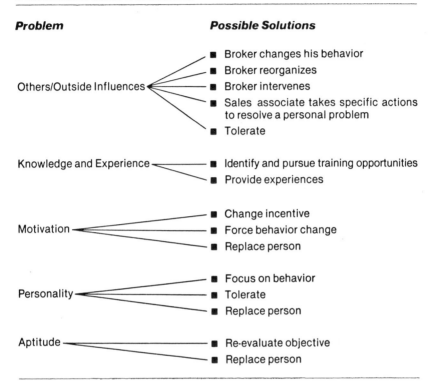

Problem

Possible Solutions

Others/Outside Influences
- Broker changes his behavior
- Broker reorganizes
- Broker intervenes
- Sales associate takes specific actions to resolve a personal problem
- Tolerate

Knowledge and Experience
- Identify and pursue training opportunities
- Provide experiences

Motivation
- Change incentive
- Force behavior change
- Replace person

Personality
- Focus on behavior
- Tolerate
- Replace person

Aptitude
- Re-evaluate objective
- Replace person

searching, realized that his own erratic approach to management was leading to confusion on the part of his staff, costing his people both time and money. In an effort to solve the problem, he created certain rules for himself. By striving to comply with these rules he is forcing a change in his behavior. It's a constant battle, but his staff is following his example and he finds himself becoming more comfortable with his new approach to his job. Another broker who finally realized his own tendency to get over-involved with the affairs of his staff has learned to control this behavior.

Solution 2: Broker Reorganizes A broker with a medium size commercial firm recognized that he was not cut out to be a manager, that he basically enjoyed sales. Many of his people's problems were attributed to his own failure to work with and manage them. He hired an office manager and continued doing what he did best, selling.

Solution 3: Broker Intervenes Sometimes the broker must take direct action to resolve a problem. One broker faced with repeated problems between the closing department and the sales offices spoke directly to all parties concerned, developing a set of priorities which, for the good of the organization, he required them to follow.

Another broker with a commercial firm discovered that several personal investments were siphoning off a considerable amount of a good salesperson's energies. He sat down with the salesperson and helped him establish a divestment plan for the problem properties. The result? The associate re–established himself as one of the firm's top producers.

Solution 4: Sales Associate Takes Specific Action By their nature some problems preclude direct intervention by the broker. An example is a family problem such as pressure from the sales associate's spouse. Having identified the problem, however, the broker can indicate to the sales associate, in a supportive fashion, that it is necessary that the person resolve the issue or minimize its impact on the sales office. Remember, a sales associate will often avoid the issue as long as he possibly can. By forcing the person to confront the issue the broker is doing the individual a favor. Ignoring the situation will usually drag out the period of unacceptable performance to the detriment of the firm.

Solution 5: Tolerate Sometimes the source of the problem is one which cannot be easily resolved, at least in the immediate future, perhaps an illness in the family. Then the broker has to ask himself the question, "Can I live with it?" If the answer is yes, the broker may choose to tolerate the situation. If the answer is no, the person should be replaced. Having identified the real problem, pep talks and other efforts at resolution are doomed to failure. The sooner both parties confront the reality of the problem, the better for all concerned.

Knowledge or Experience

The solution to a knowledge or experience problem is straightforward: suggest or provide training or the necessary experience. These solutions, it should be noted, are only effective when the problem is lack of knowledge or experience. Training will not, for example, help a motivation or personality problem.

Solution 1: Training One office faced a down market which was depressing the sales force. Financing was tough to come by. Many of the salespeople were unaware of the financing options available to them in this type of market.

Consequently, a series of training meetings were scheduled. Sources of financing and methods of qualifying and conditioning buyers and sellers under the current market conditions were thoroughly reviewed. This represents a classic training approach to a knowledge- and experience-based problem.

Solution 2: Experience The distinction between training and experience is somewhat artificial. Affording sales associates experiences which contribute to their personal development is, in a very real sense, a form of training. However, since the term training conjures up images of structured classroom activity, while experience suggests field work, we will make the distinction here. Staff development can and should transcend the staff meeting room or formal training conferences. For example, George Jones had a promising sales prospect, Jim Martin, whose performance was lagging in just one area, obtaining "for sale by owner" listings. A problem-solving interview such as we are discussing here quickly revealed that a lack of knowledge of technique was the major source of the problem. George gave the sales associate some articles to read and devoted time to the subject at the next sales meeting.

This training resulted in improved performance, although not to the extent George believed was obtainable. Yet, clearly the sales associate was trying. George decided some structured "hands on" field experience would be valuable. He accompanied the sales associate on a series of FSBO visits, sometimes demonstrating technique, at other times observing Jim's technique and making constructive comments later on. After a couple of months Jim's performance in this area was equal to his performance generally— one of the best in the office.

Motivation

Essentially, a motivation problem exists when

1. the salesperson finds certain aspects of the job distasteful or not satisfying; or
2. when something occurs which is perceived by the salesperson as threatening his ability to satisfy important aspirations.

When dealing with motivation problems, it is important that real estate brokers remember one thing: *people are self-motivated.* Motivation is not something a broker can do for the sales associate. A broker *can* create an environment which meets the needs of self-motivated people, and he can understand their problems and try to help them arrive at solutions. In other situations the broker can be supportive. But the basic motivation has to be there.

Solution 1: Change Incentives Part of creating an environment which is supportive of highly motivated people is providing the proper incentive. Remember, top salespeople are self-motivated. Highly motivated people direct their behavior toward certain things (incentives). When those incentives are missing, their performance will fall off for a short time. Usually they start searching for a more satisfying working environment, a search which may result in their leaving the firm. The astute broker will recognize and continually clarify the parts in the job environment which serve as incentives for his key people. One broker, with a medium size midwestern firm was confronted with a sales associate who was visibly upset after someone else was appointed to a sales manager's position in a new office. It was clear the sales associate was disappointed that someone else got the management position he had hoped for. In this instance the decision on whom to promote to manager had been a difficult one, since both individuals were highly qualified. However, the broker had not anticipated the extent of the disappointment of the sales associate who was not chosen.

In understanding that the sales associate wanted the opportunity to manage an office, the broker channeled the conversation along two lines.

First, he identified the kinds of activities he thought indicated managerial promise: helping other, less experienced salespeople, coming up with creative new programs for obtaining listings, etc.: in short, activities which would clearly demonstrate managerial potential.

Second, the broker established that the firm was still growing and that other management opportunities would be available.

The broker, of course, did not promise a manager's job to the sales associate. But he did specify the criteria on which the selection would be made, and, more importantly, reinforced the fact that there would be other opportunities. In doing this he offered incentive for future performance.

Another broker faced with a similar situation found it necessary to pursue a different tack. In this instance the broker felt the sales associate would not make a good manager.

First, the broker got the sales associate to agree that he was upset because the promotion went to someone who had less time with the firm than he did. Once this was out on the table and could be discussed openly, the stage was set for progress to be made. The following excerpts are illustrative of the ensuing conversation.

Broker:	John, you're one of our most successful salespeople. You're really enthusiastic about your job. What do you like most about your work?
Sales Associate:	You know the answer to that, Harry. Being responsible for myself.
Broker:	I've noticed you really like to move around. Last week for example, I didn't see you in the office hardly at all.
Sales Associate:	Well, I am out a lot. That's where the action is ....
Broker:	How much time do you think I spend in the office?
Sales Associate:	I don't know, a lot, I guess.
Broker:	More than half my time. Most of it is spent keeping track of people. Solving their problems. Do you really think you would enjoy that?
Sales Associate:	No.
Broker:	Neither do I.

This abbreviated version of their conversation presents the tenor of the solution arrived at. In talking it through, the sales associate came to realize that he was happy with his job the way it was. As a manager he would be forced to do things which he would not find satisfying; in fact, he would probably neglect many important management duties. He would not like the burden of dealing with others in a systematic, managerial fashion. In realizing this the sales associate came to better understand the incentives which were important to him. The broker, realizing the importance of the sales associate's ego, made a mental note to himself to periodically recognize the sales associate's outstanding performance.

Solution 2: Force Behavior Change It is not possible to remake a person. However, given a strong desire to succeed, people can sometimes develop certain habits which can help them improve their performance. For example, a broker may suggest a salesperson schedule a set time to make follow-up phone calls to prospects. If followed religiously, a conscious habit can be established even though the sales associate dislikes making the calls. The broker can even follow through by initially monitoring the schedule. This will only work if the manager determines that

1. the person really wants to succeed and is well motivated in other areas of the job, and
2. the person recognizes that establishing this habit pattern will greatly help his performance.

Solution 3: Replace the Person If the person is generally not motivated to succeed, or is easily defeated, the only business solution is to replace the person. Tolerating someone who is "looking for a place to hang his hat" or is "simply looking for companionship" hurts the esprit de corps of the office and, of course, increases desk costs.

Personality

A broker cannot change someone's personality. In fact, he should avoid the mistake which one broker described as "the ego trip of thinking I can remake this person." Almost every broker who has tried this has come to regret it. We can sometimes alter a certain behavior if the salesperson has the commitment to try.

Solution 1: Focusing on Behavior A salesperson can strive to tone down certain behavioral traits which are part of his personality. The key is to focus on very specific behaviors. For example, a manager of a sales office in a midwestern firm had a highly motivated sales associate with considerable potential. Her sales record was good. However, she tended to be somewhat rigid in her dealings with others. For example, once she formed an opinion of the price a seller should ask, or what a buyer needed in a house, she tended to be unresponsive to alternative suggestions. This was causing her to miss some opportunities with her clients.

Jointly she and the broker agreed that in the future, once she determined a course of action, she would ask herself "What if for some reason this won't work, what would I do next?" In other words, she would force herself to consider alternatives. She also agreed that when she felt herself resisting a suggestion from a seller or buyer, she would ask at least a couple of questions before responding. Then she would talk about what she saw as the advantages of the suggestion *before* making any negative comments. This would give her an opportunity to relax and consider the proposal in a more open fashion.

It wasn't easy, but gradually she developed some habits which toned down her inflexibility with others. And her sales performance improved accordingly. She hadn't changed her personality. But she had learned some new behavior patterns which helped her control certain aspects of her personality under certain circumstances.

Solution 2: Tolerate If the sales associate can't alter his behavior, the broker has to ask himself. "Can I live with it?" If the answer is yes, then simply agreeing to tolerate the problem is a solution. Both broker and sales associate recognize the problem and agree that if it becomes too noticeable the broker will mention it, but beyond that, the situation will be accepted. Perhaps the sales associate has other positive traits which make the trade–off worth it.

Solution 3: Replace the Person If the answer to the question "Can I live with it?" is no then the solution is straightforward. It is in the best interest of both parties for the sales associate to move on.

Aptitude

A broker cannot create aptitude. Essentially the broker has made a selection mistake. Either the broker *reevaluates the objectives* and accepts marginal performance or he *replaces the person.*

Nail Down the Next Step

Once a solution for dealing with the problem has been reached, nail down the next step. This, as we learned earlier, is important in any conflict management situation. Constructive criticism is no exception.

Agree when the solution is to be implemented. Counseling psychologists know that effective personal change is characterized by *seizing the first opportunity to implement the change.* Remember, awareness and action plans are useless unless they are translated into action. Each lost opportunity for putting a solution into effect reduces the probability that the action plan will ever be utilized.

Be fanatical about the solution. When the solution involves establishing new behavioral patterns, repetition is the key to success. Until new habits are formed, *any* exception is likely to undermine the effectiveness of the solution. Thus, until the performance problem which generated the criticism is rectified, the sales associate should strive to avoid any exceptions.

In line with the above points, the broker should indicate that he intends to *follow up* with the sales associate on progress being made. In fact, it is advisable set a follow-up date. Once the problem-solving session has ended and both broker and sales associate get caught up in the pressures of the business, it is all too easy to let the follow-up slip. Scheduling a definite time to touch bases to review the problem is a practical way of making sure the follow-up occurs.

Remember, it is difficult to change. Sometimes trial-and-error experience is necessary before the salesperson finds the required skill and confidence to make the new approach work. The follow-up date should allow for a period of experimentation—enough time for the subordinate to try out a different way of performing, but not so long that time is wasted if he encounters problems.

In establishing the follow-up date, the broker sets the stage to make it easy for the sales associate to communicate any lack of success he may have experienced. For example, the broker might say

> Even though we both believe we can put this plan into effect, it may not work out exactly as planned. If you run into difficulty, we should get together and discuss it.

At the same time, setting the follow-up date communicates the the broker's continued interest in seeing the situation resolved. It establishes that the broker is serious about the matter and doesn't want the sales associate spinning his wheels.

During the experimental period, positive feedback should be given as the sales associate attempts to change and begins to show some success. Don't wait for the formal follow-up date to give this important reinforcement.

Conducting the Follow-up Session

There are four basic parts to any follow-up discussion:

1. Discussion of what has taken place as far as the agreed–upon solution is concerned. The sales associate should be asked to describe the things he has attempted to do and evaluate them. In other words, describe what worked and what didn't work.
2. Discussion of the possible reasons why the new approach has been or hasn't been successful. Sometimes the broker and sales associate come to realize that the problem they have been trying to solve is not the real problem. In such instances the broker will once again have to use his communication skills to identify the real problem.
3. Agreeing on adjustments or revisions to the original solution.

4. Setting the next follow-up date. Again, the importance of follow-up in effecting meaningful behavior or performance changes must be emphasized. If the problem has not been completely resolved, another follow-up session will be necessary.

Guidelines for Giving Constructive Criticism

The approach outlined above is an active, involved *problem solving* approach to giving criticism. It utilizes the communication and conflict management skills previously presented. Managers who approach criticism in this fashion tend to elicit commitment and higher performance from their sales associates. Criticism becomes a vehicle for personal improvement, not embarrassment or threat. Below are some guidelines which can help the manager make the most of his efforts.

1. Don't Waste Your Time Mortimer Feinberg, a distinguished industrial psychologist, has observed that when a manager has admiration for a man's strengths and compassion for his deficiencies, he can tell him almost anything and expect him to acknowledge it. But if the manager doesn't have admiration for his strengths, he shouldn't waste time trying to improve the deficiencies.

Experienced, successful real estate sales managers echo Feinberg's point. Too often the broker invests considerable time trying to develop the marginal or failing producer. But *the payoff is in investing time with the good producer.* Once it is clear a person isn't making it, be frank about it and free your time for helping a good producer.

2. Criticize Privately People like to be recognized publicly and criticized in private. Don't embarrass staff people in front of others. Criticism should be delivered in the uninterrupted privacy of the manager's office.

3. Pick the Proper Time for Criticism Experience demonstrates that the sooner criticism occurs after the act, the more helpful it is likely to be. If the criticism involves a single undesirable act, speak about it immediately.

But be sure there is sufficient time to work through the problem. Don't squeeze someone in and then have to hurry him out. The more serious the problem, the more time should be allocated.

And try to avoid entering into a heavy criticism session right at quitting time. It is best accomplished when all parties are fresh and the conclusion of the interview will give the sales associate an opportunity to get involved in his work.

4. Don't Over-criticize Focus on the problem at hand, don't exaggerate the situation, and work on one point at a time. Criticizing several different aspects of a person's performance will confuse the issues and mask problems the broker is most concerned about. Make progress in one area first. There will be time later to deal with other issues.

5. Avoid Making Comparisons Holding one sales associate up as a model is seldom well received. Describe how the sales associate being counseled can do better without referring to others. Sales associates appreciate a manager who is helping them be better, not one who tries to make them into someone else.

Further, unfavorable comparisons tend to produce hostility within the group, undermining cooperation between members of the sales team.

6. Don't Make a Joke of the Criticism Perhaps because of the awkwardness of the situation, there is always a temptation to use a light touch. It is seldom effective.

Trying to be humorous when giving criticism can have at least three unintended consequences.

First, it can get in the way of the message by suggesting the problem isn't really a problem. A joking manner can very easily mask the fact that the broker is giving important criticism.

Second, joking can undercut respect for a broker. "He doesn't seem to take anything seriously" is not a compliment when directed toward a manager.

Third, well-intended humor can come across as sarcasm. The risks of humor outweigh the advantages. Play it straight.

Conclusion

Managing conflict, problem solving, giving criticism—these are activities which, in one form or another, have to be dealt with almost daily. The key to effective resolution rests with good interpersonal skills on the part of the broker.

Review the building block skills presented in Chapter 2. Practice each of them until you feel comfortable enough that you find yourself using them intuitively in your dealings with others.

Similarly, review the models for conflict management and problem solving and strive to integrate the skills into the recommended steps. With time and practice the real estate manager will find these models blending into his natural style, which is the highest level of skill development.

Part II
Interpersonal Communicating and the Management Process

Part I introduced a number of communication concepts and skills germane to managing others in the real estate sales office. Part II relates these skills to specific managerial activities and situations such as selection interviewing, developing and motivating the sales associate and performance reviews.

Building on Part I of the book, additional skills and models with particular relevance for these activities are introduced. The emphasis is on establishing communication processes which place the broker in control of the real estate sales office.

Chapter 5
Selection Interviewing: Sizing Up the New Sales Associate

Anyone who manages others assesses others. The most critical assessment situation which confronts the broker is the selection interview. Mistakes here cost the broker time, effort, money and lost opportunities. Recognizing this, many brokers identify staff recruitment and selection as one of the most important managerial activities in which they are involved. As one successful broker put it, "There is always a vacuum of good sales talent. Making the right choice is critical. I worry as much about the staff selections I make as anything else."

In-depth, personal interviews and tests are the primary sources of selection data on a sales applicant. Most often, the interview is pivotal in making the selection decision. Few brokers extend an offer to a sales applicant if the interview has revealed some damaging characteristic, regardless of test results. Some brokers rely entirely on the personal interview in making a selection.

Interviewing and the Selection Process

The importance of the selection interview can be clearly seen when we consider the entire recruitment and selection process, as summarized in Exhibit 10.

Most brokers report they will have at least two in-depth interviews with sales applicants, apart from the screening interview and formal testing. Some brokers require three. Often, one of the in-depth interviews will take place in the applicant's home since the sales associate's work requires a more complete integration of business activity with private life style than is the case with most other careers. Support from home is often a critical factor in the early stages of a sales associate's development. Additionally, as one broker put it, "It is more difficult for applicants to put up a pretense in their home environment. You can learn a lot about an applicant by observing him at home."

Clearly, experienced brokers have learned the importance of obtaining as much first-hand knowledge as possible about an applicant. In fact, as Exhibit 10 illustrates, information obtained through interviews directly influences at least two of four intermediate decision points in the selection process. With effectively developed interviewing skills, a broker not only collects highly relevant information, but does so efficiently, often uncovering damaging information early in the recruitment process.

The Preliminary Interview

When a prospective sales applicant comes into the office and meets the broker, remember that initial impressions are important. The broker is seeing the applicant as the prospective seller or buyer will. Observe the person carefully. Is the applicant easy to warm up to? Professional in his approach? Self-confident? How long has the person lived in the area? Most important, will he or she be able to project the image of the firm?

What about the applicant's communication skills? Does he express himself easily? If the broker indicates he really wasn't thinking of adding someone right away, or another highly qualified applicant has applied for a position, is the person discouraged or does he say he would like to be considered anyway? If the applicant appears to measure up favorably, the broker will retain his application and schedule a formal, in-depth interview.

This chapter provides tested communication methods for handling such an interview. Using the methods suggested below the broker will be able to effectively eliminate the majority of inappro-

Exhibit 10
Summary of the Recruitment and Selection Process

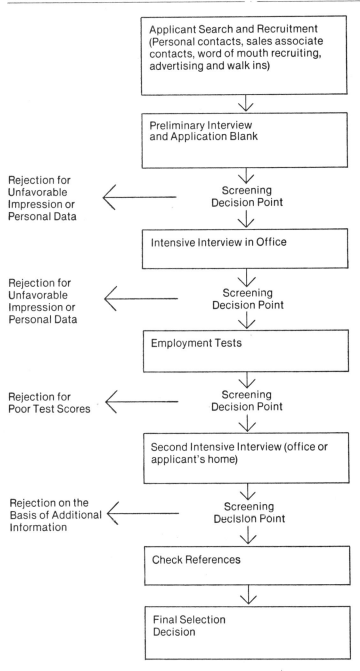

Applicant Search and Recruitment
(Personal contacts, sales associate
contacts, word of mouth recruiting,
advertising and walk ins)

Preliminary Interview
and Application Blank

Rejection for
Unfavorable
Impression or
Personal Data

Screening
Decision Point

Intensive Interview in Office

Rejection for
Unfavorable
Impression or
Personal Data

Screening
Decision Point

Employment Tests

Rejection for
Poor Test Scores

Screening
Decision Point

Second Intensive Interview (office or
applicant's home)

Rejection on the
Basis of Additional
Information

Screening
Decision Point

Check References

Final Selection
Decision

priate candidates after the initial in-depth interview.[1] By utilizing these same skills throughout the selection process, effective and confident staff selections can be made.

Some Typical Mistakes Interviewers Make

Sometimes we are quite effective in evaluating others during an interview; other times we err. The following segment of an interview illustrates the point.

Broker:	I see that you went to State University.
Applicant:	That's right. I was a business major.
Broker:	How did you like it?
Applicant:	Oh, it was all right—it's a good school and I think it's given me a good foundation for business.
Broker:	Did you go in the evenings?
Applicant:	Yes, I took two courses each semester. I started while my children were growing up. It takes a while to get your degree at night, but the instructors are good.
Broker:	You know, we are interested in people who are willing to work hard to get ahead. This business requires a lot of hard work and effort to succeed. How do you feel about working hard?
Applicant:	I want to be busy. I think you only get out of life what you put into it.
Broker:	Do you want to make a lot of money?
Applicant:	Yes, that's why I am thinking about real estate.

What is happening here? Although the broker is working hard at the interview, little reliable information about the applicant is forthcoming. If the interview continues in this fashion the broker will get only a superficial impression about the applicant. There is little likelihood he will acquire a clear understanding of how the applicant will perform.

Before considering what else the broker could have done, let's analyze what goes wrong during selection interviews. In particular, there are four common and serious mistakes which inexperienced interviewers are prone to make. Any broker should be especially sensitive to them.

1 *The interviewer talks too much.* The purpose of the selection interview is to generate information about the applicant. Unfortunately, this is not always apparent when observing a broker interviewing a potential staff person. Too often the broker is spending more time selling the firm than he is assessing the candidate.

If the broker dominates the conversation by selling the business, his firm, or discussing his own experiences in real estate, the flow of information is in the wrong direction. Further, the more the broker talks during the initial stages of the interview the more likely he is to commit the next mistake, which is to indicate to the applicant the proper response to his questions.

2 Telegraphing the "correct" answers. Often how a question is asked or the tone of voice used while asking the question sends a clear message to the applicant what type of response the broker wants. For example:

Broker:	(*speaking enthusiastically*) The great thing about this business is that you are your own boss. Your success or failure depends largely on yourself. If you're a winner you can make a lot of money and not be dependent on some corporation for it! How do you feel about being in control of your destiny?
Applicant:	That's very important to me. To be able to earn based on my own ability and to have the independence to work as hard as I need to are what I want most in a job.
Broker:	Great! In my firm, I have to have complete confidence in my associates. This business demands that I be able to take them at their word. Would I be able to do that with you?
Applicant:	Yes, without question.

In this brief exchange, we can see how the broker is setting up the answers to his questions. Only a truly insensitive applicant would fail to pick up the cues. This, of course, undermines the whole purpose of the selection interview.

3. The interviewer jumps to conclusions. In our dealings with others it is easy to be impressed with a particular achievement or personal characteristic and attribute too much or even erroneous significance to it. Unfortunately, this can happen easily in interviewing situations.

A good example of this mistake is when a broker assumes that because the applicant has been successful in other sales jobs, he or she must know a lot about the sales process, or will be successful selling real estate. Another illustration would be to assume that someone is successful because he is well dressed.

In one instance a sales applicant who had worked for a consumer products company stated on his resumé that he had made the single largest sale in that company's history. Although this was true, probing revealed he had fortuitously been assigned to a sales territory which had been well developed by his predecessor. And the "largest sale" involved a long-time corporate customer who, due to a set of unique circumstances, placed the order. This information places his accomplishment in a different light. Yet, how easy it would have been to jump to an inaccurate set of assumptions about the applicant.

4 Failing to translate facts into information. When interviewing, most brokers successfully generate an impressive list of facts about the applicant. The problem which confronts the broker is how to translate these facts into information which can predict how the applicant will perform on the job. This, we suggest, is most effectively accomplished during the course of the interview itself, where it is possible to substantiate these judgments.

Where the applicant has worked in the past, the specific nature of those jobs, past accomplishments, and who he knows in the community are illustrative of facts typically elicited during interviews. Information is what these facts tell us about the applicant's likelihood of success on the job. If an applicant has been a member of an important town commission and successful in getting controversial programs approved, what does that tell us about his potential in real estate sales? The purpose of the interview is to go beyond just collecting facts, and provide answers to such questions. In other words, the interview should provide informed judgments about the applicant's potential performance.

By following a tested interviewing format, and utilizing proven interviewing skills, the broker can avoid these and similar mistakes.

Deciding What to Talk About—The Interview Plan

Preparation is an important part of the interview process *before* the broker meets with the sales applicant. The better prepared the broker is, the more likely it is he will be in command of the interview. And the more he is in command of the interview the more relaxed both he and the applicant will be. Also, he will be less likely to miss important information during the interview.

In particular, the broker should review the candidate's application, resumé or other sources of information before the applicant arrives for the interview. Then he should develop an interview plan.

An interview plan consists of the major topics or areas of discussion the broker plans to cover during the interview. These areas may vary somewhat from one applicant to the next. Among the areas usually covered by brokers are

1. work experiences
2. school experiences (of younger applicants)
3. aspirations and goals
4. leisure time activities
5. the candidate's strengths and limitations
6. outstanding achievements
7. attitudes toward job and company

Each of these topics (and others of a similar nature) is a possible exploration area. One way to insure broad coverage in an interview is to develop a plan. The topics the broker wishes to cover with the applicant can be arranged in sequential order and discussed one at a time. By focusing on one area and exploring it thoroughly before moving on to the next, the broker systematically insures that each area receives the attention it deserves.

Although the areas covered in the interview plan may vary slightly from one applicant to the next it is strongly recommended that the broker consider including the following areas with almost every applicant. Experience indicates each area can develop meaningful information about future job performance in real estate.

Attitudes Toward Job and Company

During this part of the interview, the broker solicits and explores the applicant's feelings toward the job for which he is applying. In the case of a sales applicant, how does he feel about sales work? Does he view it as a genuine service or does he harbor reservations? How does he feel about the real estate business? The firm?

Knowing how the applicant feels about these questions is critical in making a good selection decision. Many individuals who apply for selling positions have been subjected to prejudicial views of sales work. Some even question entrepreneurial behavior. Experience clearly indicates that people who hold such attitudes do not succeed in sales. The person who unreservedly views the salesperson as providing a necessary and critical service and helping people achieve a desired end is most likely to succeed.

Of course, asking these questions directly often telegraphs the correct answer. Questions appropriate for initiating a discussion in this area include:

- *"What do you feel are the most important parts of a salesperson's job?"*
- *"What is there about sales work that is appealing to you?"*
- *"What do you see in this job that is not available in other jobs?"*
- *"No job is altogether perfect. What do you feel is the least satisfactory aspect about selling?"*
- *"What do you like least about sales work?"*

Answers to questions like these often provide real insight into an applicant's feelings about sales work. The best answers are those which communicate a positive and convincing attitude toward "putting together deals," "helping people make the right choice" or otherwise influencing the behavior of others.

Aspirations and Goals

How the applicant sees himself in the future is one of the most valuable pieces of information the broker can elicit. Successful real estate people enjoy testing themselves and believe they will succeed.

The important measure in this area is, as one broker stated, "Can they see themselves earning that kind of money?" Most applicants will feel it would be great to earn big dollars. Whether they really believe they can will determine their future success. Individuals who have given thought to their careers prior to applying for a job can usually talk knowledgeably about the direction in which they see themselves headed.

Outstanding Achievements

Behavioral scientists often observe that past behavior is the best predictor of future behavior. A broker can learn a lot about an individual's potential for future achievement by examining his past accomplishments. When discussing the applicant's achievements, the broker should be sensitive to two things:

1. The kinds of things the applicant considers an achievement. The magnitude of the accomplishment is of particular importance

because it says something about the applicant's perception of success.
2. What skills the applicant used in realizing his accomplishments. Especially important are achievements which required influencing and assertiveness skills; getting others to do what he wanted them to do. If the applicant has been successful in utilizing these skills in the past, it is likely he will succeed in the future.

Fulltime and Part-time Work Experience

When applicable, this area represents a valuable source of data on the applicant's skills and motivations. By asking questions directed toward understanding what aspects of his or her past jobs the candidate liked most and least, the broker can elicit important information on the individual's motivations and similar characteristics. Exploring why the applicant was successful in past jobs can reveal insights into her motivations and skills.

Many applicants wish to leave current jobs because of a lack of opportunity for success and achievement. What someone dislikes about past jobs can be as informative as past successes.

Identifying Critical Traits—The Emergence Approach to Interviewing

Apart from deciding which discussion areas to cover during the interview, the broker must determine which of the applicant's personal traits and characteristics he intends to examine while following the interview plan. The problem here is to choose from the many facets about people which seem tantalizingly interesting when it comes to predicting job performance. To illustrate this point, I asked several brokers to list the traits or characteristics they felt were critical to learn about when assessing an applicant. The following list emerged:

self–confidence	self–discipline
aggressiveness	ambition
social perceptiveness	energy
enthusiasm	persistence
interest in people	ego
ability to communicate	poise

If a broker could accurately gauge the applicant along each of these characteristics the probability of making a good selection decision would be high. However, assessing someone across such a broad range of characteristics during the course of an interview is problematical, even for professional interviewers. Further, addressing these characteristics directly often telegraphs the proper answer.

An interviewing method which has been growing in popularity among professional interviewers since the early 1970s has particular application for REALTORS®. Called the "emergence approach," it allows the interviewer to create a discussion in which the dominant characteristics of the applicant emerge naturally during the conversation.[2] Rather than set out to assess the applicant against a list of predetermined traits or characteristics, each applicant's unique profile evolves during the interview. This approach provides the broker not only with an understanding of which key traits are present in the applicant, *but also provides insight into how the applicant has applied these traits in past situations.* This, of course, is the key to predicting future job performance.

The broker compares the unique combination of traits which have emerged during the interview with those personal characteristics he feels can lead to success in his firm. If several important traits are absent, the decision will probably be against offering a sales position to the applicant. On the other hand, the presence of several important characteristics indicates a promising salesperson.

For the emergence approach to be used effectively, however, the broker must be sure that all aspects of the applicant's makeup have an opportunity to emerge during the interview. This can be accomplished by covering four factors during each piece of the interview plan.

The Four Basic Assessment Factors

There is a long list of characteristics and traits which can potentially comprise an individual's makeup. However, virtually all of the ones relevant to predicting job performance can be classified under one of four basic factors. If the broker has accurate information about the applicant in all four factors, he will be basing the selection decision on his assessment of the "whole person."

1. Motivation Simply defined, motivation is what a person *likes* to do. In assessing future job motivation, the broker needs to determine the kinds of activities and situations an applicant has found satisfying in the past. If the pattern of activities the applicant has enjoyed in the past is similar to the critical activities he must perform as a sales associate then the likelihood of motivated performance is high.

In the case of a REALTOR-ASSOCIATE® dealing with strangers,

Exhibit 11
The Four Factors of Selection Assessment

In assessing an applicant the broker needs to learn about the person's

1. *Motivation* - what he likes doing and what he aspires to.
2. *Knowledge and Experience* - skills and knowledge he brings to the job.
3. *Personality* - his most salient personal characteristics and traits.
4. *Intelligence* - the person's basic ability level.

___

putting together deals, and influencing the decisions of others are illustrative of possible satisfaction patterns which may predict success.

Another aspect of motivation is *aspiration*. If what an individual is working toward can be achieved through success on the job, then motivation is likely to be high.

2. Personality As a practical matter, personality refers to specific behavioral traits and temperament. From a broker's standpoint, this means determining how the applicant will fit into the work environment and how he will get along with others. Is he aggressive? excitable? rigid? friendly? ... and so on.

Of particular interest to the broker with a small or medium–size firm is how the applicant will fit into the organization. In the competitive atmosphere of a real estate sales office, compatibility is an important consideration. This is not to suggest that every successful applicant be cut from the same piece of cloth. However, it is important to determine how the applicant will relate his unique personality to his colleagues' in the work environment. The broker will want to be reasonably certain the candidate will contribute to a climate of cooperation in the office.

A special note is appropriate here. It sometimes happens that during a selection interview a broker has a vague feeling of uneasiness with an applicant, but cannot put his finger on anything specific about the person which is disturbing him. Under such circumstances the broker should trust his feelings. These feelings are often rooted in intangible but real cues which emerge during the discussion. Brokers who fail to heed such feelings because they think them too subjective, often regret having done so.

In every instance the broker should eliminate the applicant with extreme personal characteristics which are likely to grate on his co-workers and clients. Acquiring diversity of this nature seldom proves to be an asset to the firm.

3. Knowledge and Experience This factor is relatively straightforward. Is the applicant's job-related knowledge and experience sufficient for him to take hold and become established along a learning curve which will lead to success? The broker must establish the minimum level of knowledge and experience which, in his judgment, is necessary for success. Included under this factor is level of formal education. Another important consideration is the personal life experiences of the applicant. One highly successful sales manager observed that mature sales associates are able to establish empathy with buyers because they have experienced or are experiencing the same life situations as their clients: disruption caused by corporate moves, pressures of being cooped up at home with small children or problems of re-entering the job market. Common experiences are an important basis for establishing effective sales relationships. The smart broker looks for these experiences when assessing a potential associate.

4. Intelligence This is the fourth factor which needs to be explored by the broker during the interview. The broker need not attempt to measure the level of intelligence beyond establishing that the individual is sufficiently alert to grasp the essentials of the business. Rather, it is *applied intelligence* which is critical.

Is there evidence that the applicant will use his abilities in a manner conducive to job success? For example, is he likely to be creative in coming up with methods for obtaining listings or showing houses? Will he know where to seek financing in a changing market? Or, will he be quick to see an angle which might make a property attractive to a prospect?

If after the applicant leaves the interview the broker can comfortably discuss the individual's motivations, key personality characteristics, knowledge and experience level and how the applicant applies his intellectual abilities, then the broker will be in a position to make an informed selection decision. During each segment of the interview plan, the broker's objective is to learn something about each of the four factors. By doing so he is likely to leave the interview with a thorough knowledge of the applicant.

A method for accomplishing this objective is our next topic.

A Model for Conducting the Selection Interview

Prepared with an interview plan of the topic areas he intends to explore, the broker is ready to begin the interview. Exhibit 12 outlines a step-by-step model for conducting a successful selection interview. If followed, the model can help the broker implement his plan in such a way that meaningful information on each of the four factors emerges from the discussion.

Step 1—The Opening

A good opening is critical to the success of the interview. Well handled, the opening sets the tone for the remainder of the interview while avoiding the more typical interviewing mistakes. The broker seeks to accomplish two things during the opening:

1. Place the applicant at ease.
2. Establish the structure of the interview.

1. Placing the applicant at ease The more relaxed the applicant is during the interview, the more likely he is to share information which provides insight into his true characteristics and motivations. One of the best ways to relax the applicant is to make sure he is comfortable. Have a place where he can easily hang his top coat. Offer a cup of coffee. The broker should sit alongside the applicant, and not conduct the interview across a desk.

While it is natural to engage in pleasantries as the applicant is getting settled, avoid extended, manufactured small talk. Remember, the applicant is eager to talk business, too. Take control of the situation by explaining what is going to happen during the interview.

2. Structuring the interview The broker's opening remarks should inform the applicant how the broker wants the interview to proceed. In the process, the broker can structure his role in such a fashion that he retains control of the interview. For example, the broker might say:

"Sue, your application suggests you might be the kind of person who can make a real contribution to our firm. This morning I would like to learn more about you so we can make a decision which is right for both of us. First, I want to spend some time asking you questions and getting to know you better. Then, I'll be happy to answer any questions you may have about our firm. To start with, tell me something about ..."

An opening like this:

Exhibit 12
A Model for Conducting the Selection Interview*

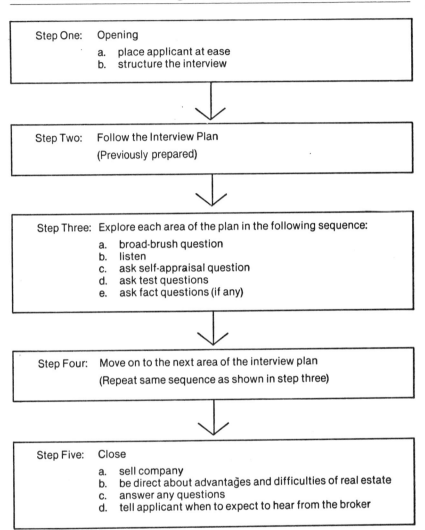

Step One: Opening
   a.   place applicant at ease
   b.   structure the interview

Step Two: Follow the Interview Plan
             (Previously prepared)

Step Three: Explore each area of the plan in the following sequence:
   a.   broad-brush question
   b.   listen
   c.   ask self-appraisal question
   d.   ask test questions
   e.   ask fact questions (if any)

Step Four: Move on to the next area of the interview plan
             (Repeat same sequence as shown in step three)

Step Five: Close
   a.   sell company
   b.   be direct about advantages and difficulties of real estate
   c.   answer any questions
   d.   tell applicant when to expect to hear from the broker

*Adapted from John Drake "Interviewing for Managers" Op Cit.

- lets the applicant know that her initial impression has been positive, which is why the interview has been scheduled.
- structures the interview. First the broker intends to ask the questions; then the applicant will have an opportunity to discuss her concerns.

- leads into the body of the interview while avoiding a lengthy explanation which might establish a pattern of the broker talking too much.

Notice the above opening avoids offering a detailed explanation of either job responsibilities or the firm's policy and organization. Early in the interview detailed explanations not only get the broker instead of the applicant talking, but often lead to questioning by the applicant. Such a role reversal is exactly what the broker is striving to avoid. Additionally, the more the broker talks about the firm, the more likely he is to send cues which "telegraph" the right answer to future questions.

Remember, the applicant already has a general idea of what the job involves. The broker can go into detail just as easily later on in the interview, after he's determined how interested he is and therefore how much time he wants to invest in the applicant.

Step 2—Follow the Interview Plan

Once the broker has opened the interview, he should follow the previously established interview plan. Each area should be thoroughly discussed, with the broker attempting to learn as much as possible about the applicant, and then moving on to the next discussion area of the plan. Start the interview with an area which should be easy for the applicant to discuss. This will help in putting the applicant at ease. For example, "Tell me something about your background" is preferable to "Tell me how you see yourself in five years."

Step 3—Explore Each Area of the Plan in the Following Sequence

Professional interviewers know that to be successful in generating meaningful data they must systematically explore each area of the interview plan. Random discussion seldom generates useful information.

The heart of any interviewing system is the effective use of questions. Questions are the interviewer's tools, and as with any set of tools, different kinds are needed for different purposes. With practice, a broker can learn how to use certain questions so that pertinent pieces of information are elicited from the applicant to make up a meaningful whole. Four kinds of questions are used during the selection interview:

- broad brush questions
- self-appraisal questions

- tested questions
- fact questions

Each is a refinement of the open-ended questions discussed in Chapter 2.

Broad Brush Questions Broad brush questions are used to open each area of the interview. A broad brush question is a very general, open-ended question which invites the applicant to comment on any aspect of the topic he chooses. For example, a broker exploring an applicant's work history might begin with the broad brush question, "Suppose you tell me something about your current job." If the applicant should ask, "What in particular do you want to know?" the broker can simply say, "Anything you like."

The broad brush question has many advantages. First, it doesn't telegraph to the applicant what information is important to the broker. Second, it invites the applicant to talk at length and removes the burden of conversation from the interviewer. Third, while accomplishing the above, it makes it easy for the candidate to begin talking about whatever he is most comfortable with within the general constraints of the topic. Finally, the interviewer will learn something from what the applicant chooses to discuss. For example, a high achiever will most likely comment on some of his job accomplishments. A chronic complainer will often talk about how unfairly he was treated on his last job. A nice, but low achiever, may just focus on how pleasant the place was to work.

Once learned, the broad brush question is a straightforward and easy way of introducing each discussion area of the interview. The most common mistake is to phrase the question in terms which are too specific, thus focusing the candidate's attention on a particular aspect of the topic. To test your understanding of this concept, try your hand at Exercise 5-A at the end of this chapter.

Listening Once the applicant responds to the broad brush questions, the broker's task is to listen. Listening, as discussed in Chapter 2, is active—not passive—involvement with what the applicant is saying. The broker wants to continue drawing out the applicant by using the listening skills learned in Chapter 2. The problem is similar to conflict management, but instead of learning more about how the applicant perceives or feels about a situation, the broker is learning about the applicant's capabilities and past performances.

Follow up on the candidate's response with an *open-ended question,* a question which invites the applicant to tell more about the subject at hand and which can't easily be answered yes or no.

Use *expanders* occasionally to express interest in what the person is saying with good eye contact, nodding the head and so forth. Responsiveness on the part of the broker is likely to relax the candidate and encourage him to expand on his answer.

When the applicant is involved in what he is saying, the best response is to *restate* in a simple declarative statement the key idea he has been expressing. Most often this encourages the individual to elaborate on his comments.

Remember, don't dominate the conversation. Ask a question and wait for the answer. When the broker continues talking after asking a question, he almost always telegraphs a good answer. Silence is a critical skill in selection interviewing.

Consider the following segment of an interview, using the skills discussed thus far:

Broker:	Suppose you tell me something about your current job situation.
Applicant:	What in particular are you interested in?
Broker:	Anything you feel is important.
Applicant:	Well ... (*broker, not interrupting the pause, but observing how the applicant reacts*) I am a customer service representative at the _____ Company. In that job, you are continually dealing with the public, usually when they have a complaint or a problem. One of the things I enjoy is turning an irritated customer around. They come in with their minds made up and it's a challenge getting them calmed down and leaving happy.
Broker:	(*restating*) You like satisfying an upset customer.
Applicant:	Yes, half the time the problem's their own fault. You can't just tell them that, though. First you have to get them thinking you understand and care about their side. Empathy. That's the key. When you empathize with people you can usually get them to look at their situation differently.
Broker:	(*restating—looking attentive*) You relate to people well.
Applicant:	Yes, I've had fewer customer problems turned over to my supervisor than anyone

	else in the department. My supervisors have always commented on how good I am in getting people to change their mind.
Broker:	It sounds like you are a success at your job. What has you thinking about a change?
Applicant:	The fact that I am so good, but get the same money everyone else gets. Salary increases are pretty well fixed and advancement is based on seniority. I can't see myself going any place. I think I have real ability and it's being wasted. I feel buried working for someone else.

Compare this interview segment with the one we read at the beginning of the chapter. Although the broker has asked fewer questions during this segment, he is further ahead in eliciting meaningful facts and impressions about the applicant.

Self-appraisal Questions Once the applicant is talking, the broker will learn many facts about the person: events, occurrences and claims about skills which are subject to verification. For example, in the interview segment above, the broker found out the applicant is: a) experienced in dealing with the public, b) is rated highly by his superiors in job performance, and c) has been successful in influencing others.

As an interviewer, the broker's problem is evaluating these facts. What do they tell us about the person in terms of job performance? How should the broker interpret the facts? In other words, the facts have to be translated into information.

Suppose an applicant says, "I was the sales leader in my district for the past three years." How are we to interpret that fact? If we stop to think about it, several possible explanations come to mind. Among them are:

- the applicant is a hard worker
- the applicant is ambitious
- the applicant is a good salesperson, a "natural," or
- the applicant had a district with several established customers.

Which one is correct? Well, it is hard to tell unless we ask a *self-appraisal question*. A self-appraisal question is one which asks the candidate to explain what a fact means. In effect, a self-appraisal question says to the applicant, "Tell me how I should interpret what you have just told me."

For example, to continue with our illustration of the district sales leader, the broker might ask, "How do you account for your success in selling?"

He might answer, "Well, I have always put in a lot of hours. I find you have to service the accounts to get the orders."

Now we can make a more intelligent guess about what the fact means. He's a hard worker. By repeatedly following up on the critical facts with self-appraisal questions, the broker increases the probable accuracy of his judgments about the individual.

Self-appraisal questions are effective because they require the applicant to go beyond simple description of their past experiences and provide explanations for them. Few people come into an interview with "canned" answers for these kinds of questions. The broker should be prepared for many applicants to fumble over their answers and be less polished than when they are describing themselves at a more surface level. Use of *expanders* by the broker to demonstrate acceptance and understanding can help keep the applicant relaxed during these kinds of questions. If the applicant feels he is doing well he is more likely to talk freely.

Exhibit 13 provides several examples of self-appraisal questions. Completing exercise 5-B at the end of this chapter will give you practice in phrasing self-appraisal questions.

Tested Questions Earlier we said there are four basic factors which the broker wants to cover in each area of the interview plan: motivation, knowledge and experience, personality and intellectual ability. As the broker uses the listening skills and self-appraisal questions to focus on increasingly specific aspects of the area of the interview plan being discussed, characteristics pertinent to each factor are likely to emerge. However, by asking *tested questions* the broker can be sure he has made an effort to cover all the factors during each area of the plan.

A tested question is an open-ended question which directs the candidate's answer toward one or two of the factors. For example, "What do you like most about your current job?" is going to direct the candidate's answer toward the motivation factor. Exhibit 14 gives illustrations of typical tested questions used by REALTORS®.

We recommend that a broker develop a couple of tested questions for each area of the interview plan. If these or similar questions do not come up in the course of the interview, ask them before moving

Exhibit 13
Examples of *Self-appraisal Questions*

1. What was there about *(job, town commission)* that you liked?

2. How would you evaluate yourself as a salesperson? What skills do you have which might account for your success?

3. You said that you were *(chairman, town representative)*. What do you think there is about you which led your *(fellow committee members, associates, neighbors)* to pick you rather than someone else?

4. To what do you attribute your success in ....?

5. You said you have ambitions to *(earn money, etc.)*. What is there about yourself that makes you feel you can succeed at ....?

on to the next area of the plan. In this way, the broker can be sure he has touched on all the factors.

Fact Questions Once the broker has asked any tested questions, he can ask any additional fact questions on points he wishes clarified. "I see from your application you have been with your current employer since 1974. Were you in sales for all of that time?" The broker is then ready to move on to the next area of the interview plan.

Step 4: Move On to the Next Area of the Interview Plan

Having completed his exploration of the first area of the interview plan, the broker is ready to discuss the second. Once again the broker should repeat the same sequence of broad brush questions, listening, self-appraisal questions, tested questions and fact questions. Then the broker moves on to the next topic area of the interview plan. In this fashion, the interviewer systematically generates information about the applicant.

Broad brush questions make the transition from one discussion area to the next flow smoothly as in a natural conversation. For example, the broker might say, "I am interested in your activities away from the job as well. I see from your application you are active in civic affairs. Tell me something about your work on the town recreation commission."

Exhibit 14
A List of Tested Questions

A tested question is a question which will most likely provide information on one or two of the four basic assessment factors:
Motivation
Personality
Knowledge
Intelligence

Every broker should develop a list of such questions which he includes in every interview to insure that all the factors are covered. The questions below are examples.

		M	P	K	I
1.	Tell me about your greatest success.	x			
2.	What kind of people do you like to work with?	x	x		
3.	How many hours a week do you expect to work?	x			
4.	What kinds of sales work have you done?			x	
5.	What are your income goals?	x			
6.	What are some things you find difficult to do?				x
7.	How did you get through college?	x			

Or if the broker wanted to explore what personal contacts the applicant has, he might introduce this area with a question like:

"Tell me something about the acquaintances you feel might be useful to you in real estate."

If the broker follows the recommended sequence of questions he will find he averages 10 to 15 minutes on each area of the plan. Thus, a thorough selection interview might take more than an hour. It will be an hour well spent as the broker collects valuable information prior to making a critical personnel decision.

Step 5: Close

Once the broker has covered each segment in his interview plan, he is at Step 5 of the model. If he is interested in the applicant, the broker should spend some time selling the company to the applicant. After talking with him in such depth the broker will be in a position to emphasize the points which the broker knows are important to him.

Also, answer any questions the applicant may have. Although wanting to sell a promising candidate on the advantages of the firm, the broker should be frank about the difficulties of succeeding in the business. The truly promising candidate will not be discouraged.

In closing, emphasize your interest in the applicant and tell him you will be in touch within the next day or two. If the firm uses a testing service, have the applicant complete the test. After the interview is over, the broker should carefully consider the applicant, using the techniques and methods discussed in the remainder of this chapter.

Organizing Notes

Following the model described above will result in a considerable amount of information on the applicant. The broker will want to record that information in a format which facilitates the selection decision.

First of all, it is recommended that the broker take notes during the interview. Without notes, the broker will forget a lot about the applicant, even if he makes notes right after the interview. If the broker keeps his pad tilted so the applicant can't see what the broker is writing, and writes evenly throughout the interview, note taking will not disrupt the interview process. Stop writing every once in a while. This will get the applicant wondering what he has just said.

The simplest, most effective way to take notes is to divide your notepad in half. On the left side, jot down facts. On the right side, jot down what you think the facts mean. Not every fact will have a corresponding interpretation; only those which have been followed up with a self-appraisal question. This means there will be more notations on the left side than on the right. Exhibit 15 illustrates how a typical notepad might look. Notice each notation is a concise memory jogger of the point in question.

The right side of the pad consists of the broker's hunches, or interpretations of the facts collected from the applicant. A good interviewer will collect 30 to 50 such interpretations in the course of an interview. Remember, each interpretation is an "informed guess" about the individual, generated from self-appraisal and test questions. The broker can also include judgments about the individual derived from careful observation during the interview.

Exhibit 15
Illustration of a Typical Notepad During a Interview

Fact	Interpretations
— Lived in area five years	
— Member of town committee	
— Has had six town bills pass the committee this year	Likes to be in control of events
— Has always been active in community organizations	Seeks personal recognition

This approach to note-taking will feel awkward at first. With practice, however, the broker can expect to become quite proficient with the technique.

Making the Selection Decision

At the conclusion of the interview only half of the broker's job is completed. The broker still has to utilize the information obtained to make a good selection decision. A thorough, productive interview is wasted if the broker fails to use the data at his disposal.

A Balance Sheet Approach

A useful tool in making the selection decision is the applicant balance sheet.

As suggested above, following the interview the broker will edit his notes, retaining only those impressions or interpretations which have received substantial support during the interview. These retained interpretations can be used to develop a balance sheet on the applicant. On one side of the balance sheet the broker lists the applicant's strengths; weaknesses are listed on the other side. With the strengths and weaknesses summarized in this fashion, the broker can think more effectively about the candidate. Consider the balance sheet of a sales applicant's interview illustrated in Exhibit 16. Would you reject the applicant or consider him a strong candidate?

Exhibit 16
Illustration of a Balance Sheet from an Interview with a Sales Applicant

Strengths	Limitations
Quick thinker, bright and alert	Impulsive - tends to act before thinking
Energetic	Can be rigid in his thinking
Good motivational pattern. Has overcome resistance from others.	Tense - excitable
Makes good impression, warm and ingratiating.	Inclined toward being disorganized
Neat appearance	
Good level of drive — a self starter	
Seems insightful regarding others	

Actually, this balance sheet was developed from an interview with a highly successful sales associate. As such, it provides a few lessons about evaluating candidates.

When evaluating someone, expect to find weaknesses. In fact, since everyone has weaknesses, absence of any weaknesses on the balance sheet probably reflects a poor interviewing job. So the broker shouldn't be overly concerned about the weaknesses. Rather, it is the combination of strengths and weaknesses which is important.

Guidelines for assessing an applicant's balance sheet are:

- *Do the applicant's strengths counterbalance his weaknesses?* For example, an applicant may appear to be overly impulsive and too likely to make snap judgments. If, however, the applicant is also very alert and smart, this particular weakness is less of a problem, since many of his snap decisions are likely to be intelligent ones; whereas, an impulsive but slow thinker might make snap judgments which could prove disastrous for the firm.

- *Can the weaknesses be overcome or controlled?* Many times, with proper management, one can overcome or neutralize a weakness. The broker may feel that an applicant who is disorganized might moderate this weakness by conforming to certain controls. If the applicant appears open to such direction from the broker, then the weakness can be managed. Lack of real estate experience is regularly overcome by training.
- *Most important, are the proper strengths present?* If the critical characteristics the broker feels are necessary for success are not present, then the selection decision is no. The issue is not simply the presence of strengths, but the proper ones for the firm and the job in question. The presence of the *proper* strengths carries considerable weight toward a yes decision.

Using Person Specifications

An applicant's strengths should be matched against a set of person specifications which have been developed by the broker for the job in question. Although based on a job description, person specifications describe a person, not a job. Essentially, they spell out those personal characteristics considered by the broker to be essential for job success. A set of person specifications should exist prior to beginning the interviewing process. Once developed, a set of person specifications can be used whenever the broker is interviewing candidates for that particular job. However, the broker will probably continue to make modifications in the specifications which reflect his experience with past selection decisions. Indeed, careful and continued analysis of the kinds of individuals who succeed within the firm is one of the beneficial managerial activities a broker or sales manager can engage in.

When developing person specifications the broker should describe the successful applicant in terms of the four factors of motivation, knowledge and experience, personality and intellectual ability. Then if the broker follows the interviewing model presented in this chapter he will be sure to develop data relevant to the person specifications. If the strengths which emerge from the interview correspond closely to the predetermined person specifications, the broker knows he has a strong candidate. Should the dominant characteristics which emerge during the interview be significantly divergent from the person specifications, the broker has strong reason to believe the applicant would not work out. Exhibit 16 presents a set of person specifications for a REALTOR-ASSOCIATE®.

Guidelines for Developing Person Specifications

Although it is generally agreed that certain characteristics typify the successful sales associate, the specific person specifications are likely to vary somewhat from one firm to another. Firms vary in their markets, typical clientele and in the climate or atmosphere the broker wishes to achieve in the firm. Indeed, some branch offices of the same firm vary according to these characteristics. Therefore, it is recommended that each broker and branch manager invest time in creating a set of person specifications.

Motivation Factor Consider the activities the sales associate (or clerical person) must consistently be involved with on the job. Based on this analysis, describe what the successful applicant must like to do—or at least not dislike. What career aspirations are most needed for each position?

Personality Factor Describe the specific ways the applicant will have to interact with others.

Knowledge and Experience Factor What specific knowhow and experience are truly necessary?

Intellectual Factor What kinds of judgments will the successful applicant be capable of making?

A Word on References

Out of the above process will emerge one or more attractive candidates whom the broker feels can make a meaningful contribution to the firm. Before finalizing any independent-contractual or employment arrangement, however, the broker should always check the applicant's references. In fact, if the applicant appears attractive, the broker should begin checking before the final interview. Although many brokers might doubt the value of such an exercise, this practice can help avoid serious and unnecessary mistakes.

References are especially useful in verifying facts. By checking references you can make sure the applicant has actually had the responsibilities and achieved the accomplishments he claims. Verifying these facts is important since your judgments about the applicant rest on them. Generally, references are reluctant to volunteer opinions which may injure someone's employment chances. Therefore, beyond fact verification it is often difficult to generate reliable information on an individual. However, you can get the most from your efforts if you:

- Call and speak to the reference. You will pick up things in conversations which won't be put in a letter.
- Avoid asking questions which can be answered yes and no. For example, instead of "Is he reliable?" ask, "What can you tell me about his reliability?"
- Even when verifying facts, avoid telegraphing the right answer. Instead of asking, "Bob claims he was a district sales leader. Is that right?" Ask, "What can you tell me about his sales performance?"
- Have a specific list of questions ready before contacting the reference.

Once the broker has decided to accept an applicant, critical communication centers around orienting and training the new associate. These topics are considered in the next chapter. Unsuccessful candidates should be notified of the decision as soon as possible, with the broker expressing his belief that the decision was in the best interest of all concerned. The broker should also thank them for their interest and wish them the best of luck in the future.

Continuing the Selection Process

If the comparison between the applicant's balance sheet and the person specifications is favorable, then the broker will want at least one additional interview as part of the continuing selection process. While the tenor of this interview will be different, the same skills are needed.

Once more the broker will want to identify certain additional areas which, based on test results, notes from previous interviews or any other sources, he wishes to explore. The same questioning skills will apply.

Subsequent interviews will differ now in two ways: First, the broker will generally want the interview to be somewhat less structured. Apart from exploring additional topic areas, an important objective is for the broker to generate a second impression of the applicant in a more sociable setting. Interacting with the applicant away from the office often accomplishes this best. For reasons previously mentioned, many brokers interview applicants at home. Other brokers invite them to their home or meet them at a club or other such place.

Second, the broker will be more direct in describing the business to the applicant. Following the first intensive interview, the broker has a good knowledge base of the applicant. Now he is in a position to test the reactions of the applicant to the specifics of how the firm operates. In the process of doing this the broker will learn something about how the person will be to work with.

Now that the successful applicant has been selected, the broker needs to maintain the effective lines of communication which have been established. In fact, the quality of communication during the next couple of months is critical to the applicant in establishing himself in the job. To invest considerable energy in selecting good people only to let them "sink or swim" on their own makes no sense for the broker who is trying to build a viable organization. Management's communication strengths need to grow if the firm is to prosper.

Summary Checklist for Selection Interviewing

Preparation

- review application
- review person specifications
- develop an interview plan
- identify tested questions for each area of plan
- allow for 45 minutes of uninterrupted time

Conduct the interview

- opening
  - brief
  - structure roles
- follow interview plan
- explore each area of the interview plan in the following sequence:
  - broad brush questions
  - listen
  - self-appraisal questions
  - test questions
  - additional fact questions
- move on to the next area of the interview plan (repeating above sequence)
- close
  - sell firm
  - answer questions
- evaluate the candidate
  - develop balance sheet
  - compare balance sheet with person specifications
  - check references
- make decision to reject or continue the selection process

Exercise 5-A
Asking Broad Brush Questions

Broad brush questions are very general, open-ended questions, often used to introduce a new topic area during an interview. For each of the following interviewer's questions, use a checkmark to indicate whether it is broad brush or specific. If it is not broad brush, convert it into a broad brush question covering that general area.

	Broad Brush	*Specific*
1. Tell me something about your achievements on your last job.	_____	_____
2. Tell me something about your goals and ambitions.	_____	_____
3. Do you enjoy assuming responsibility?	_____	_____
4. What do you think you'll like most about real estate?	_____	_____
5. Tell me something about your community activities.	_____	_____

Exercise 5-A
Possible Answers to Broad Brush Questions

Below is indicated whether a question is broad brush or specific. Where a question is specific, we have provided a possible answer as to how it might be rewritten in a broad brush fashion.

	Broad Brush	*Specific*
1. Tell me something about your achievements on your last job.		X

Tell me something about your last job.

| 2. Tell me something about your goals and ambitions. | X | |

| 3. Do you enjoy assuming responsibility? | | X |

What things do you think you would enjoy most in your work?

| 4. What do you think you'll like most about real estate? | X | |

| 5. Tell me something about your community activities. | X | |

Exercise 5-B
Practice in Asking Self-appraisal Questions

A self-appraisal question is one which asks the applicant to explain some fact or interpret some statement for the interviewer. Below are eight statements that might have been made by an applicant in a selection interview. In the blank lines that follow each statement, write the self-appraisal questions you would use to elicit further information.

1. I made quota every year with Acme Company.

   Interviewer's self-appraisal question _____

   _____

   _____

2. I made the largest single sale in the history of our company.

   Self-appraisal question _____

   _____

   _____

3. I don't like a boss looking over my shoulder.

   Self-appraisal question _____

   _____

   _____

4. I've always been interested in sales work.

   Self-appraisal question _____

   _____

   _____

5. I am frequently complimented on my ability to deal with people.

   Self-appraisal question _____

   _____

   _____

6. I don't like a lot of paper work in a job:

    Self-appraisal question _____

    _____

    _____

7. I didn't like being secretary to three people at the same time.

    Self-appraisal question _____

    _____

    _____

8. My previous boss and I didn't get along.

    Self-appraisal question _____

    _____

    _____

Exercise 5-B
Possible Self-appraisal Questions

1. I made quota every year with Acme Company.
   Interviewer's self-appraisal question: *"That's very impressive. How do you explain your success with Acme?"*

2. I made the largest single sale in the history of our company.
   Self-appraisal question: *"Excellent. What did you do to make the sale?"*

3. I don't like a boss looking over my shoulder.
   Self-appraisal question: *"What is there about you that makes you dislike close supervision?"*

4. I've always been interested in sales work.
   Self-appraisal question: *"What is there about sales which you find so satisfying?"*

5. I am frequently complimented on my ability to deal with people.
   Self-appraisal question: *"How do you explain your success with people?"*

6. I don't like a lot of paper work in a job.
   Self-appraisal question: *"What is there about paper work that you dislike?"*

7. I didn't like being secretary to three people at the same time.
   Self-appraisal question: *"What was there about that situation which you disliked so much?"*

8. My previous boss and I didn't get along.
   Self-appraisal question: *"I guess we all run into people with whom we don't get along. What was there about this person which made it difficult for you to work with him?"*

Footnotes for Chapter 5

1. In developing this chapter the writer owes a special debt of thanks to John Drake (John D. Drake, *Interviewing for Managers* [New York: AMACOM, 1972]). The author has been a close colleague of Dr. Drake's and has found his research and methods invaluable in analyzing the selection interviewing problems of REALTORS®.

2. John Drake has been a pioneer of this approach to interviewing.

Chapter 6
Developing and Motivating the Sales Associate

Sound selection techniques are important to the successful and progressive development of any firm. However, while the selection decision represents the culmination of one set of communication efforts the communication process between broker and associate is just beginning. It makes little sense to invest time and energy selecting good people, only to neglect them once they become associated with the firm. The "sink or swim" method of orientation increases the probability of turnover, with loss of high potential associates.

Real estate is a high turnover industry. Estimates of turnover range from "a conservative 30 percent to as high as 70 percent."[1] Most of this turnover occurs during the first six months. Yet, if a broker is attempting to build an organization which is an important factor in the local market place, it is imperative that he retain a stable core of professional REALTOR-ASSOCIATES®.

The first year in a career is critical in any industry. It is especially crucial in the increasingly competitive area of real estate. Once the broker realizes that he has several specific opportunities to help the high potential recruit become established he is ready to begin *managing* his turnover.

Orientation and Training

Managers in most industries today recognize that proper orientation and training impact both on a person's *ability* to do the job and his *attitude* toward it. The basic objective of training is to provide an individual with the knowledge and skills which lead to competent job performance. Additionally, when the firm takes positive steps toward helping the new staff person become as skilled as possible in performing his job, positive attitudes toward the firm are established. A formal training program gives management a chance to teach not only methods of doing the job, but also a spirit or approach toward the work. In other words, training familiarizes a new associate with the ways of the firm, as well as developing skills.

Training Resources

There is a wide variety of resources available for training the new sales associate. In choosing materials it is important to consider such factors as 1) how accessible the resource is, 2) how flexible it is in terms of application (i.e. can it be used in combination with other resources), and 3) how cost effective it is (i.e. amount of knowledge or training received v. the cost per person trained). The broker should think in terms of developing a set of training resources which he can offer to sales associates.

Developmental resources can be classified into the following categories:

1. Readings With few exceptions, most knowledge and skill areas have had at least one book or article written which provides pertinent information for the new sales associate. Readings are easily and readily accessible, are flexible in terms of application (they can be used in combination with other types of training resources such as direct coaching by the broker or as discussion points during sales meetings) and are very cost effective.

The broker can build a library in which there are catalogued books and articles of particular help to the developing sales associate. One broker in the southwest maintains a topical reference library of books relevant to real estate sales. Additionally, he periodically obtains reprints of good articles and catalogues them under special headings for easy staff reference. New sales associates are given a recommended schedule of readings. Experienced sales people are periodically referred to new material. Not surprisingly, this broker's associates have a reputation for being especially well informed as well as proficient.

2. Interviews with relevant professionals Lawyers, lending officers, public officials and the like are another group of developmental resources. One firm has its new people interview a lawyer, a mortgage officer, spend five to six hours with an experienced sales associate and visit the deed recorder's office and a local title company as part of their first week's orientation. The experience of actually meeting these individuals is one of the best methods of helping the new sales associate understand his new occupational environment (and remember, understanding is what communication is all about). After each visit, the sales associate discusses what he has learned with the manager.

3. Media (audio-visual material) There are a number of films and video tapes on sales technique available from both the REALTORS NATIONAL MARKETING INSTITUTE® and film rental libraries. They are both specific and general in application and can be used effectively in combination with readings and coaching.

As with readings, tapes, films and slides are flexible and cost effective. Since they require the use of play-back equipment they must be used at the office. However, the advantage these materials have is one of dramatic emphasis.

4. Professional education programs A number of Marketing Institute Courses specifically designed to improve the real estate professional's knowledge and skill base are available nationally. They lead to the REALTOR-ASSOCIATE® earning a designation of proficiency in his field and are among the most systematic and thorough of the training resources available.

5. Sales meetings Sales meetings provide a natural vehicle for continuing education within the firm. Periodically scheduling meetings which either refresh old skills or develop new ones (i.e., obtaining financing in tight markets) is a valuable use of both staff and management time. Such training meetings can be scheduled in connection with readings or media aids. Experienced staff can provide pointers and outside lecturers may be scheduled. In addition to providing valuable job skills, a sense of team spirit can emerge from the training meetings (see *Real Estate Sales Meetings*[2]).

6. Developmental coaching On-the-job coaching is an oft-cited technique for improving knowledge and skill. Perhaps there is no better way to develop the sales force than direct instruction from the broker. It is often the most readily available resource; yet it is often overlooked.

On-the-job coaching brings the broker into direct communication with the sales staff. This kind of communication is relatively easy since the broker is only confronted with two basic problems:

- the most effective way of initiating and conducting the coaching, and
- insuring that the investment of time is most productive.

Let's examine more closely what experience teaches us about how to handle this type of communication.

Methods for Effective Coaching

In describing a coaching method it might be helpful to indicate that, depending on the objective, the broker can adopt one of two basic roles: First, if the broker wishes to teach or simply impart knowledge, he can adopt a "telling" or "instructing" role. Second, if the broker wishes to assist in the sales associate's growth, and does not have anything in particular he wishes to teach, he can assume a "helper" role. Let's analyze each of these two roles in more detail.

The "Telling" or "Instructing" Role

When the broker wishes to communicate information to help train or develop a sales associate, he can communicate in a fairly direct manner. For such a discussion to be effective only two basic conditions need exist. First, the broker must know more about the subject at hand than the sales associate. Second, the sales associate must be willing to accept the broker's judgment. Whenever these fundamental assumptions are met, the broker can coach in a teacher-student posture.

Within this posture there are certain rules of thumb which can facilitate the coaching process. Basically, the steps of effective instruction are as follows (incidentally, this approach is effective any time the broker is describing a new task, including giving instructions to the clerical staff):

Step 1: Indicate the end result Begin the instructional session with an explanation of what is expected as an end use and result of the task or activity being taught. For example, when explaining how to write contracts, the broker should first discuss why a completed contract is important, how the contract is used later in the closing process, and the kinds of problems a well-written contract can circumvent. Or, if teaching how to complete certain required reports such as phone contacts, the place to begin is with how this information is used (both now and later) and why.

Unfortunately, many managers explain things with only a superficial discussion of the end result. This inhibits the sales associate's (or clerical staff's) understanding of the procedure or job he is learning. It also limits the number of questions which may occur to the listener. An understanding of the end result often helps us to formulate questions.

Step 2: Explain whatever it is the broker wishes to convey Thus, a step-by-step explanation of the task at hand is the second and not the first step of the process.

Experience in training indicates that most people learn best if the task is taught step-by-step. For example, a broker trying to teach a sales associate how to convert "For Sale by Owners" into listings, might break the technique into steps or stages, teaching the principles and techniques associated with each step:

- Get into the house.
- Sell the owner on how a broker would be beneficial.
- Sell the firm as the best one to represent him.

Once the sales associate has learned to perform each step, he can then practice all three together, perhaps through role play. Psychologists refer to this as "first part, then whole learning" and it is a very effective approach to training. Incidentally, the step-by-step models in this book are another illustration of part, then whole learning.

Step 3: Provide concrete examples Wherever possible, examples of what is being taught should be provided. When teaching how to complete contracts or other paper work, samples of forms or materials should be given. In training sales techniques, video demonstrations of technique can be used along with verbal instructions. Trainers have long known that visual and verbal instruction is superior to verbal instruction alone. In fact, films and video tapes are best used as part of the coaching process as opposed to being the primary vehicle for training.

When teaching skills, such as gaining an interview with a potential lister, the broker may want to demonstrate the skills. Modeling the proper approach is one of the most effective methods of teaching. The broker may invite another member of the staff to role play the adversary so he can demonstrate the approach being taught. For example, many brokers model telephone technique by using two office phones in a role play format.

Step 4: Summarize Summarizing what has been taught reinforces the whole concept.

Step 5: Ask other person to feed back what he learned This is a critical step, but one which is often overlooked. Much conflict and many problems in firms are caused by simple misunderstanding. Before leaving the coaching situation, ask the sales associate to restate what he has understood. It is only through this feedback that the broker can know the extent to which his information has been communicated.

Unfortunately, most of us simply ask "Any questions?" This is not good instructional technique. All too often the other person says no and then goes out and makes a mistake.

Reflect for a moment on why people often fail to ask important questions:

- They don't want to appear stupid.
- They think they understand, and questions only come to mind once they start trying to do the job.
- They just can't think of any questions.
- They misunderstand you, but aren't aware of it (remember, people's perceptions lead to different interpretations).

By asking the sales associate to repeat his understanding of what should be done, the broker provides the best possible check on the communication which has taken place. The process of feeding back what has been learned often stimulates questions or brings to light misunderstandings. And, of course, if the person doesn't understand, he will have to ask questions.

In fact it is good managerial practice to go through this step whenever you have explained a significant change in procedure or have introduced someone to a new task. Don't worry about offending the other person. Simply saying something like, "To be sure we have the same understanding, why don't you briefly describe how you would handle this?" is never resented—especially since it usually results in some important clarification of what has been learned.

When teaching a sales technique, such as handling objections, it is often useful to have the sales associate role play the skills. Training experts know the value of role play and its use is standard technique in management development programs. Role play provides the sales associate with a safe environment in which to practice his skills, while at the same time making it possible for the broker to critique and coach his performance.

Role play is simple to create. Simply have another, preferably seasoned, member of the firm play the potential seller or buyer. The sales associate being trained has to achieve some objective, such as obtaining a home interview or a listing. This arrangement makes it possible for the broker to observe the sales associate's technique. After the role play is over the broker can descriptively feed back his observations (for example, "In response to the objection, 'We aren't ready to sell,' you said . . .") and thus effectively coach the associate.

Step 6: Schedule a follow-up Soon after the sales associate has had a chance to use the information which has been imparted, chances are that once he starts trying to do what has been explained some questions or problems will arise which were unresolved and which he may hesitate to ask about. Most sales associates do not like to say, "I don't understand." They often hope they can figure out on their own what is puzzling them. For example, perhaps a particular sales technique is not working out the way it should. A follow-through, however casual, will often encourage the person to ask questions. Then the broker can help resolve the situation.

There is no magic in the above approach to teaching. It simply recognizes the natural points where instructional communication tends to break down and encourages straightforward steps toward avoiding those problems. It is the lack of a systematic approach to the coaching effort which often renders it ineffective.

The Case of John and Sue

Misunderstandings happen easily. Consider the case of John Brown, broker, and Sue Johnson, one of his new sales associates. Sue is talking to her husband at dinner: "Sometimes I wonder if John really knows what he wants. During our sales training he made a big deal out of not having the closing and taking possession on the same day. He talked on and on about the hassles which are created for the buyer who has to worry about getting to the bank and then the physical move. 'Therefore', he said, 'don't accept the closing and possession on the same day.'

"Well, the other day I had a buyer who insisted on closing and taking possession the same day. I stood my ground and the buyer went elsewhere. When John found out about it he called me in and said not to push the issue so strongly that I lose the sale. 'You have to use some common sense,' he tells me. What it sounds like to me is that he wants one thing in theory and another in practice."

Meanwhile, John is telling his wife, "Sometimes I wonder what goes through people's minds. You know how I always tell my salespeople to try to avoid having the buyer close and take possession on the same day? Well, Sue really took it to extremes. The other day she had a buyer who insisted on closing and taking possession on the same day. She refused to accept it. As a result, she lost the sale for the seller. What gets me is she thought she did the right thing. When I told her to use some common sense, she looked at me as though I was crazy."

What's happening here? Clearly, Sue feels that she did what she was told and now John is changing the rules of the game. For his part, John feels Sue really didn't do what he expected. The result is a typical example of a boss-subordinate misunderstanding.

Forget for the moment that in discussing the matter with Sue it seems that John failed to utilize the problem solving models we learned in previous chapters. How might the misunderstanding have been avoided in the first place?

In retrospect, John admitted that he never asked for feedback from Sue after explaining this particular sales technique to her. Had he done so, John felt they would most likely have had a conversation which would have clarified the conditions which Sue needed to take into consideration when setting a closing date. John also felt that, had he done a better job of explaining the end-results first, Sue would have asked more questions.

It's easy for misunderstandings to occur when the broker is explaining the job to others. Following the steps of the telling role can minimize their occurrence.

The Helper Role

One of the greatest favors a broker can do for one of his people, particularly if the person has potential, is to invest time in helping him capitalize upon his abilities. *All too often a broker permits his time to be dominated by the marginal performer, whereas it is the high–potential, strong producer with whom he should be spending time developing a relationship.* This can be accomplished by creating a climate of trust and understanding so that the sales associate will share his feelings about such topics as *areas for skill improvement, his future in the company, and his concerns about his present performance.*

In the helper–type discussion the broker is attempting to respond to the concerns of the salesperson. Much communication follows from what the broker wants to discuss, such as resolving performance problems, giving feedback and instructions. In the helper role the topic of communication is determined by the sales associate. By initiating this type of discussion the broker is principally interested in what the other person has to say. This discussion needn't be a formal procedure; in fact, it's best if it isn't. A casual discussion is best. However, the broker's principal problem will be to listen and not dominate the conversation.

In any conversation a clear understanding of what is expected helps people focus their thoughts. Therefore, the broker might initiate the discussion with an introductory comment such as:

> I like to take time out now and again to see if I can help people develop themselves further. I have no specific comments in mind, but I am wondering if there are any ways I can be of help to you?

If the sales associate declines the offer of help, the broker does not want to push the point too far. However, since the other person might not have given the matter much prior thought, the broker might explore the matter a little further by asking a few questions. If the sales associate indicates interest in pursuing the discussion the broker is in a position to work with the issues the sales associate raises.

It is important that the broker avoid the temptation to lecture. The idea of the helping role is to encourage the sales associate to express problems and feelings which may not be immediately evident to the broker. Remember, if the broker has something specific to tell the sales associate he can either adopt the "telling" approach described above or utilize the conflict management and problem solving skills discussed in Chapters 3 and 4.

Once the sales associate brings up a topic and the broker has explored it at some length (to assure that the associate's own diagnosis of his needs is correct), a decision can be made as to what, if anything, should be done about it.

Sometimes it will be difficult to think of ways the broker can be of help. Thus, after discussion of a particular topic, it might be helpful to review a checklist. One such list, now in use in one firm, is found in Exhibit 17. Discussion of each item may generate a number of ideas that might be useful in helping the sales associate.

Exhibit 17
On-the-job Development Possibilities

Some actions an individual can take to develop:

- Practice special skills (role play)
- Plan his reading
- Plan each work day more carefully
- Visit branch offices
- Observe others; when appropriate, use them as models
- Develop presentations for sales meetings
- Attend professional development courses and workshops
- Ask manager for more frequent feedback on performance
- Be more critical of his own work

When discussing plans of action, it is also helpful to consider the question "What is going to be done differently tomorrow that will make possible the improvement we want?" It is far too easy for both parties to agree on generalities such as "I'm going to look into that. . ." with the result that nothing is accomplished. Nail down the specific next steps and set a definite date to review progress. Development is a continuing process that needs readjusting and encouragement.

Through such "helping" conversations, the broker can solidify a close working relationship with the sales associate.

Motivating the Sales Associate

"How can I motivate my people?" is a question often asked by managers. Experienced sales managers know that the question is misleading. Strictly speaking, managers don't motivate their people. People are *self*-motivating.

The residential sales manager of a large firm in the western United States told me that over the years he has learned that "most good salespeople seem to pull themselves out of slumps." "They don't stay down for long." As he talked, he went on to observe that these people have a strong, intrinsic desire to succeed. Another office manager of a midwestern firm put it this way: "Good sales-people don't have prolonged slumps; they have self-healing ups and downs."

These managers put their fingers on a critical point about motivating others: sales managers can and must provide the rewards which accompany accomplishment, but the desire to obtain the reward must be already present. In other words, *people are essentially self-motivated.*

In making this observation, we don't mean to suggest that the sympathies and words of encouragement which every successful broker finds themselves providing are unimportant. However, the essential contribution which this type communication maintains is a certain level of satisfaction within the organization. Certainly, it can provide a boost to an individual's morale. At minimum it provides a feeling of caring and helping people over the rough spots. At other times it can help a sales associate deal with a non-motivation based performance problem (i.e., others—outside influences or personality). But it doesn't *motivate* them. Satisfaction is not the same as motivation. We have all met many satisfied people, who were not motivated. This suggests that the broker must establish priorities for his time. Once the broker recognizes that a sales associate is characterized by a strong desire to succeed, the broker's time is best invested in working with this individual rather than trying to generate motivation where it doesn't exist. As one sales manager stated it:

> Some of the biggest mistakes I've made
> with people involved trying to prove I
> could turn someone into a motivated sales
> person. I think it was an ego trip for me;
> a challenge to prove I could do it. Always
> these people created problems for me
> which usurped my time.

This does not mean that motivation is irrelevant to managing others. Managers are confronted with motivation-related problems all the time. To be successful in resolving these kinds of problems, it is important for the broker to understand how he influences the motivation of his sales associates.

Looking at Motivation

Virtually every management text dealing with motivation published during the last 20 years makes reference to Abraham Maslow's hierarchy of needs. Maslow's theory has been a central statement directing research into the needs of individuals as a basic motivating force of behavior.

Maslow identified five basic levels of needs:

1. Physiological needs (the need for food, water, air, rest, and so on)
2. Safety needs (the need for security)
3. Belongingness needs (the need for social acceptance)
4. Esteem needs (the need for feeling of achievement and recognition, etc.)
5. Self-actualization needs (the need for feeling the realization of one's potential)

Maslow argued that some needs are more basic than others, and the more basic needs (physiological) must be satisfied before higher level needs become motivators. In other words, behavior is motivated by the most basic, unsatisfied need. Thus a hierarchy is formed with physiological needs at the base of the hierarchy and self-actualization needs at the top.

While Maslow's need hierarchy makes intuitive sense and seems to explain much about human behavior in the work situation, today we know that people have many more than five needs. Maslow's categories are very general and include at each need level several very specific needs. For example, esteem needs can take the form of achievement needs, exhibitionism needs, autonomy needs or power and dominance needs. Belongingness needs can take the form of affiliation needs or nurturance needs to name but a couple. And these needs don't necessarily conform to a hierarchy.

However, Maslow's work is pivotal to an understanding of motivation, because it clearly explains that motivation is intrinsic to the person. All behavior is by definition motivated! A manager doesn't create motivation; it is already there in the form of needs. What a manager can do is 1) recognize the needs of his people and 2) create a work environment which meets or satisfies those needs.

As a practical matter, this means three things to the brokers:

1. The broker must first identify those people whose needs for achievement, recognition, and esteem are strong enough to sustain them in a highly competitive, fluctuating business. The others are best directed down other career paths. Some people find their way into real estate whose strongest motivations are not right for success in the field. Some may have a strong need for security and thus be subject to depression when things go wrong. Others may be more motivated by affiliation needs, and while enjoying the camaraderie of the office lack the drive for personal success. Rapid determination of these motivations is in the best interest of both the broker and the other person. "Hangers-on" sap resources from the

broker and the firm while accomplishing little or nothing for themselves. This, of course, is an argument for strong initial selection procedures and close observation of newly-appointed sales associates.

2. The broker must come to understand what is truly important to his highly motivated people. To do this, he must *listen* to them.

3. The broker must respond to what he hears and create the kinds of rewards and work environment valued by his people.

To put the matter simply, managers have motivation problems for one of two reasons:

- First, either the person's motivations are wrong for the firm or
- Second, the firm's reward system is not appropriate.

Salespeople, indeed all members of the firm, expect to get certain rewards from their association with the firm. Some of these rewards are of a fairly tangible nature. Money, promotion, fringe benefits and status symbols are all examples. Psychologists refer to these kinds of tangible rewards as extrinsic rewards. Less tangible rewards are also important, such as a feeling of competence in one's work and the personal respect of one's boss and colleagues. These are generally referred to as intrinsic rewards.

The power of both extrinsic and intrinsic rewards are rooted in the personal needs of the individual. Both are important in channeling the motivation of the sales associates.

A Variety of Ways to Meet Needs

Meeting the needs of the solid and high producer is a creative undertaking. Bonus plans, million dollar clubs, private offices, cars for the top producers, trips, company-wide awards, recognition ads in newspapers and promotion into executive status are all methods for rewarding strong producers.

So are the less tangible things, such as providing secretarial support, asking producers to lead sales meetings and soliciting their input on certain appropriate management decisions.

Most importantly, brokers must realize that decisions taken in other parts of the business often have motivational consequences. This is especially true in terms of intrinsic rewards. For example, establishing a thorough training and continuing education program does more than simply insure high professional skills, as important as that goal happens to be. It also generates a feeling of competence in one's work, which industrial psychologists know is an intrinsic need in most people. Developing an organized advertising campaign, strict adherence to high ethical standards and generally creating an image of integrity and honesty in the community are all business decisions which affect the professional image of the firm. These decisions also impact on the motivation of the staff. Association with a firm which has a solid reputation in the community is a strong intrinsic reward.

There is no single "correct" technique for motivating behavior; rather, the answer lies in each broker coming up with a system of rewards which works for his company. In managing the reward system the broker must consistently balance two somewhat conflicting pressures. First, all sales associates must be eligible for the same rewards. To do otherwise is to give preferential treatment to certain people. On the other hand rewards must be administered in a manner which recognizes the individual differences between people. To do less is to create a bureaucracy, the impersonal nature of which defeats the purpose of the reward system. Thus the broker must be flexible even as he is being consistent.

Building Teamwork

In meeting the needs of individuals the broker will want to administer the reward system in a fashion which fosters cooperation among members of the sales team. Rewards shape people's behavior. Unwittingly a broker may administer rewards in a fashion which encourages success of one at the expense of others. For this reason above all, it is important that every salesperson who reaches specific standards of excellence be rewarded, not just those who get there first or achieve the most.

Good salespeople will compare themselves to others and will want to be the best. This kind of competition is natural and positive. However, if the broker creates a situation where only the best win and the others lose, a destructive and counter-productive type of competition is created.

For example, one firm had a small group of top salespeople who continued to improve in performance, and a considerable number of average producers who did not seem to be living up to their potential. This particular firm encouraged competition among sales associates through quarterly contests with prizes and benefits going to the top producers. While such rewards were effective in influencing the top performers, the impact was minimal on the average salesperson who felt he had little chance in competition with the "stars."

In this instance, the same people won all the awards every year. No matter how much the others improved, the top producers still did better. In time, the system created a certain apathy among the other members of the sales team.

Altering the performance indexes so that self-improvement was emphasized as well as top individual performance had a strong positive effect on many of the average performers. These individuals began to strive to improve their performance. This firm has learned an important lesson. *Competition with oneself is as important as competition with others, because in competition with oneself everyone can improve his position.*

An Expectancy Theory Approach

Research indicates that people with strong achievement needs perform best when there is a reasonable chance that their effort will be rewarded. In fact, research suggests that high achievers perform best when there is about a 60 percent chance of success. If the odds for success are much greater than 60 percent the sense of accomplishment is undermined by the relative ease of the task. Odds below 60 percent imply a strong possibility of failure. And failure would not result in need gratification. It seems achievers gravitate toward tasks which they perceive to be moderately difficult, but not so difficult as to be almost impossible.

Research into achievement motivation attempts to demonstrate that people anticipate what the rewards of their work efforts are likely to be. Many psychologists argue that recognizing this represents the most sensible way of thinking about motivation. This viewpoint is generally referred to as expectancy theory.

Essentially expectancy theory holds that:

1. The sales associate has preferences among the various rewards (both extrinsic and intrinsic) which are potentially available.
2. The sales associate has expectancies about the extent to which increased effort on his part will result in higher job performance.
3. The sales associate also has expectancies about the likelihood that certain rewards will accompany high performance.
4. In any situation, the motivation of the sales associate is determined by the expectancies and the preferences he has at the time.

Simply put, expectancy theory states that a sales associate prefers certain rewards, calculates the likelihood of receiving those rewards and behaves accordingly.

Expectancy theory encompasses everything we have discussed about motivation and suggests certain critical points which a broker must be concerned about in administering the reward system.

First, as we have stated repeatedly, the broker must understand and be sensitive to the preferences of his people.

Second, the broker must continually emphasize that effort will lead to success. Part of this emphasis involves providing sales associates with the skills to do the job through continuing training efforts. Another part is demonstrating that the firm is working with the sales associate in full support of his efforts. Still another part of this emphasis is retaining only those sales associates in whose abilities the broker has unquestioned confidence.

Industrial psychologists often state that high job performance = motivation x ability. Ability can be further divided into sufficient skill to perform and sufficient aptitude for the job. By providing strong professional development opportunities and not tolerating individuals of questionable aptitude, the broker brings the issue into clear focus. The ability piece of the equation is being handled by the firm. Only individual motivation stands between the sales associate and success.

Third, it must be clear that success will be rewarded. In fact, recognition should follow accomplishment as immediately as possible.

Developing Managers

Our discussion has highlighted the interdependencies between the needs of people, strong sales training programs and motivated job performance. Underlying this discussion has been the assumption that the broker is a good communicator, that he can apply the skills discussed earlier in this book to understand, respond to and, where necessary, confront the needs of his people.

It seems appropriate to stress the need for manager training. Many firms have strong sales training efforts, but leave management development to chance.

The growth pattern is a common one. An outstanding salesperson decides to open his own firm. He takes on a couple of strong salespeople and as the business grows, the broker finds himself managing others. Maybe continued growth makes it necessary to hire a manager or two. Typically, these managers are some of his most successful sales associates. Suddenly the broker is an executive managing managers who deal with his people. All are removed from the primary sales role, which perhaps is the position with which they are most comfortable and in which they excel.

In discussing his firm, a sales manager in the southeast stated "We invest a lot of time in training our salespeople. I think they are much better prepared than the competition. Our managers are another story. Their training is haphazard, almost non-existent. Unfortunately, the manager jobs are offered to the top sales producers, which sometimes is a mistake." Not surprisingly this firm, until lately successful and expanding, now is experiencing problems getting new branches established.

Managers must be selected as carefully as are new sales associates. And the sales "superstar" is not always the best managerial candidate. Often the star performer is motivated by the independence of the sales role and would not be truly happy saddled with heavy office responsibilities. Often the motivation for these individuals in accepting jobs as managers is fulfillment of an ego need: the prestige of the title. Yet, there are other ways of meeting these ego needs through awards and even the creation of quasi-executive functions, such as identifying these individuals as expert resources for the managers in certain technical areas. Unfortunately, too many brokers offer managerial slots or even "sell" them to the star performer, without sitting down and jointly deciding whether the person would *really* enjoy and succeed in a managerial role.

Certainly a sales manager should have been successful in sales but there are other characteristics which are equally important. A natural tendency toward working with and assisting others is one such characteristic. One successful broker looks for sales associates who tend to nurture and assist new associates as potential managers. Obviously these individuals get satisfaction from helping others succeed and are likely to be motivated by this aspect of the manager's role.

The ability to listen to others and to be flexible is another important managerial characteristic. So is the willingness to let others bask in the spotlight of success. This last characteristic is especially important if the new manager is going to direct achievement-oriented salespeople who bring strong motivation to their work.

Once the new manager is selected, a systematic training effort must be embarked on. There are skills to be developed, such as the ones discussed in this book. How to interview, manage conflict and solve performance problems—these are skill areas in which every manager should receive training. Other skills such as planning, time management, budgeting and sales promotion should also be part of every manager's training program. This training can be provided within the firm or from outside resources, but it should be done.

Managers, like new sales associates, are on a learning curve, and the broker should avoid placing them in a position where they feel they ought to be succeeding like experienced managers from the first day on the job. The "sink or swim" method is no more effective with new managers than it is with new sales associates.

Remember, in a growing firm, managers are the crucial linchpins in the communication chain. Systematic skill development is imperative.

Exercise 6-A
Analyzing Your Development and Motivation
(Coaching) Practices

Sometimes it is helpful to take a careful look at our development and motivation practices. The following questionnaire has been designed to help you do this. Each question can be related to a specific aspect of our coaching practices. First complete the questionnaire, then consult the analysis sheet which follows.

A similar questionnaire which asks sales associates the same questions *about you* is also provided. It might prove interesting to have them complete it and then discuss their answers with them. If you do this, emphasize you want them to be as honest as possible.

Use the questionnaire to trigger a brainstorming session on how office coaching practices might be improved.

My Coaching Practices[3]

INSTRUCTIONS: For each statement below, decide which of the following answers best applies to you. Place the number of the answer in the box at the left of the statement. Please be as honest as you can.

5. Usually   4. Often   3. Sometimes   2. Occasionally   1. Rarely
   (almost   (about half
   always)   the time)

1. ☐ I keep my sales associates informed about our overall organizational plans and operating results.

2. ☐ I keep my sales associates informed on how I feel about their performance.

3. ☐ I provide support and backing to my sales associates.

4. ☐ I express my concern to my sales associates whenever they don't achieve expected results.

5. ☐ I am accessible to my sales associates and easy to talk to, even when I am very busy and under pressure.

6. ☐ I have thorough discussions with my sales associates to help them learn from their successes and failures.

7. ☐ I talk with my sales associates about their ambitions and aspirations for the future.

8. ☐ I encourage my sales associates to participate in setting goals and determining how to achieve those goals.

9. ☐ When I talk with my sales associates about their performance, I am very open and frank in telling them what I think.

10. ☐ I provide encouragement to my sales associates whenever they are undertaking difficult assignments.

11. ☐ I praise my sales associates whenever they achieve a significant result.

12. ☐ I try to understand my sales associates' viewpoints when I discuss problems and undertakings with them.

13. ☐ I provide opportunities for my sales associates to broaden their experience and increase their competence.

14. ☐ I explain to my sales associates the requirements they would be expected to meet to qualify for larger responsibilities within our organization in the future.

15. ☐ I clarify with my sales associates their duties, responsibilities and the important results they are expected to accomplish.

16. ☐ I work with my sales associates in developing agreed-to "standards of performance" to use in judging the results they have achieved.

17. ☐ I contribute ideas (tactics, strategies, approaches, etc.) to my sales associates to help them do their jobs.

18. ☐ I provide appropriate recognition and rewards to my sales associates for the results they have achieved on the job.

19. ☐ I encourage my sales associates to express themselves openly, even when their views differ from mine.

20. ☐ I chat with my sales associates about ways they might improve their effectiveness on the job.

21. ☐ I discuss with my sales associates specific things they might do to better qualify themselves for taking on greater responsibilities in the future.

Analysis Sheet for My Coaching Practices

INSTRUCTIONS: Place the number you selected in the box at the left of each statement. Work down the sheet. Next, add the numbers across, for each set of three boxes, to determine your totals. A perfect score for a given activity is 15. The higher your score for a given activity, the stronger you are in that particular aspect of staff development and motivation. Pay particular attention to those activities which have scored low relative to the others. How can you improve in those areas? Also, how do your answers compare with those of your sales associates? Discuss their answers with them item by item. A frank discussion can lead to improved management on your part.

Activity	Totals
Goal Setting	□ 1. + □ 8. + □ 15. = □□
Performance Feedback	□ 2. + □ 9. + □ 16. = □□
Providing Assistance	□ 3. + □ 10. + □ 17. = □□
Motivation	□ 4. + □ 11. + □ 18. = □□
Working Relationship	□ 5. + □ 12. + □ 19. = □□
Continuing Development	□ 6. + □ 13. + □ 20. = □□
Future Growth and Advancement	□ 7. + □ 14. + □ 21. = □□

My Sales Manager's Coaching Practices

INSTRUCTIONS: Below are 21 statements which describe actions real estate sales managers or brokers may take in coaching their sales associates on the job. Review each statement and then decide which of the following answers best applies to your sales manager or broker. Place the number of the answer in the box at the left of the statement.

5. Usually does this (Almost always)	4. Often does this	3. Sometimes does this (About half the time)	2. Occasionally does this	1. Rarely does this (Hardly ever)

1. ☐ My sales manager keeps me informed about our overall organizational plans and operating results.

2. ☐ My sales manager keeps me informed on how I'm doing on the job.

3. ☐ My sales manager provides support and backing to me.

4. ☐ My sales manager expresses his displeasure and concern to me whenever I don't achieve expected results.

5. ☐ My sales manager is accessible to me and is easy to talk to, even when he is very busy and under pressure.

6. ☐ My sales manager has thorough discussions with me to help me learn from my successes and failures.

7. ☐ My sales manager talks with me about my ambitions and aspirations for the future.

8. ☐ My sales manager encourages me to participate in setting goals and in determining how to achieve those goals.

9. ☐ When my sales manager talks with me about my performance, he is very open and frank in telling me what he thinks.

10. ☐ My sales manager provides encouragement to me whenever I am undertaking difficult assignments.

11. ☐ My sales manager praises me whenever I achieve a significant result.

12. ☐ My sales manager tries to understand my viewpoints when he discusses problems and undertakings with me.

13. ☐ My sales manager provides opportunities for me to broaden my experience and increase my competence.

14. ☐ My sales manager explains to me the requirements I would be expected to meet to qualify for larger responsibilities within our organization in the future.

15. ☐ My sales manager clarifies with me my duties, responsibilities, and the important results I am expected to accomplish.

16. ☐ My sales manager works with me in developing agreed-to "standards of performance" to use in judging the results I have achieved.

17. ☐ My sales manager contributes ideas (tactics, strategies, approaches, etc.) to me to help me do my job.

18. ☐ My sales manager provides appropriate recognition and rewards to me for the results I have achieved on the job.

19. ☐ My sales manager encourages me to express myself openly, even when my views differ from his.

20. ☐ My sales manager chats with me about ways I might improve my effectiveness on the job.

21. ☐ My sales manager discusses with me specific things I might do to better qualify myself for taking on greater responsibilities in the future.

Analysis Sheet for My Real Estate Sales Manager's Coaching Practices

INSTRUCTIONS: Place the number you selected in the box at the left of each statement. Work down the sheet. Next, add the numbers across, for each set of three boxes, to determine your totals. Notice which activities are low scoring relative to others. Your sales manager will want to explore ways of putting more emphasis on those activities.

Activity   *Totals*

Goal Setting   ☐ 1. + ☐ 8. + ☐ 15. = ☐☐

Performance Feedback   ☐ 2. + ☐ 9. + ☐ 16. = ☐☐

Providing Assistance   ☐ 3. + ☐ 10. + ☐ 17. = ☐☐

Motivation   ☐ 4. + ☐ 11. + ☐ 18. = ☐☐

Working Relationship   ☐ 5. + ☐ 12. + ☐ 19. = ☐☐

Continuing Development   ☐ 6. + ☐ 13. + ☐ 20. = ☐☐

Future Growth and
   Advancement   ☐ 7. + ☐ 14. + ☐ 21. = ☐☐

Footnotes for Chapter 6

1. *Real Estate Office Management: People, Functions, Systems* (Chicago: REALTORS NATIONAL MARKETING INSTITUTE®, 1975), p. 123.

2. *Real Estate Sales Meetings: Techniques and Topics* (Chicago: REALTORS NATIONAL MARKETING INSTITUTE®, 1976).

3. *Exercise 5-A was adapted from "My Coaching Practices" questionnaire, George Truell, Williamsville, N.Y. by permission.*

Chapter 7
Appraising Performance

In real estate the bottom line is performance. More than in almost any other industry the newcomer must perform quickly and then continue to perform. Real estate is an entrepreneurial business, and there is no living off yesterday's performance either for an individual or a firm.

In this environment the most critical communication focuses on performance. Moreover, it is to the broker's advantage to be in a position to manage the performance of his salespeople. Simply giving people targets and hoping most of them hit them is not enough. A sensitive manager wants to be in a position to influence the final results. Management texts refer to this as *feedforward* or *steering* control: making adjustments during the performance period while there is still time to impact on the final, year-end results. A performance appraisal system structures the type of communication necessary for this kind of control in a business like real estate.

Simply put, performance appraisal

refers to the methods through which a broker evaluates a sales associate's performance and then communicates this evaluation to the individual concerned. Properly conceived and used, a formal performance appraisal system can do much to structure effective broker-sales associate communication. A performance appraisal system impacts on both the development and the motivation of the sales associate. At the same time it provides an objective framework for dealing with performance problems. Thus it can be an integrative force between the motivation of the sales associate and the performance goals of the firm. In fact, the answer to the question "Why have a performance appraisal system?" is strikingly simple: it structures the kind of communication between broker and salesperson that is crucial to continued performance. As one broker put it, "Working with people is important. Although top people are self-motivating, the purpose of talking with them on a regular basis is to surface the problems they may be having. I find appraisals accomplish two purposes: I can help them deal with problems and it lets them know I know how they're doing. They like to know I know and they like to hear it."

Two things characterize successful appraisal systems:

1. Appraisals are totally integrated into the performance and development of the firm. Appraising performance should not be just one more thing a broker has to do. When a broker is appraising performance, he is doing an important part of his job. A good appraisal discussion will conclude with both the broker and the sales associate feeling their time has been spent productively.
2. Paperwork is kept to a minimum. The only paperwork required should serve the purpose of documenting information needed for future reference, nothing more. The quality of the discussion, not paperwork, determines the effectiveness of an appraisal system.

Performance Appraisal Is a Process

Performance appraisal is a continuing process, not an isolated event. The key elements of the process are

- specific goals
- frequent progress reviews
- summary appraisal

Goal Setting

Successful people set goals for themselves. Goals give people targets to shoot for, concrete reminders of what they hope to accomplish.

Further, goals become measures against which they can assess their progress. When people exceed their goals they are encouraged to establish more challenging objectives. On the other hand, when they find themselves falling short, they have to assess why.

For the manager, having people commit to specifically written goals provides an objective basis for discussing performance.

Basically there are two kinds of goals:

- Job performance goals
- Personal development goals.

Job performance goals state specific levels of performance to which the sales associate is committed. Examples might be hours of work, number of listings, sales and income. Personal development goals reflect commitments to professional development and growth on the part of the salesperson; obtaining the CRS (Certified Residential Specialist) designation, for example.

Sales associates should commit to at least one personal development goal. Achieving a good personal development goal this year generally translates into achieving a more ambitious job performance goal the next.

Setting too many goals should be avoided. It is better for a sales associate to set five or six goals which are significant and, if achieved, add up to a successful year, than to write ten or fifteen goals which cover every conceivable area. When there are too many goals they tend to be left in the drawer. Goals should reflect the salesperson's most important priorities for the coming year.

How to Set Goals

Goal setting should be a process marked by mutual agreement between the broker and the sales associate. Prior to the goal setting discussion, the broker should inform his sales associates that he will be meeting with them to set goals. This can be done in a group setting, possibly at a sales meeting. In such a meeting, the broker can share with his people why he believes goals are important, how they will be used, and the areas in which he wishes goals to be developed. The broker should emphasize that goals should be neither easy nor excessively difficult. Rather, the goals should be *stretch goals*, meaning that the goals are realistic, although achieving them will require hard work. Finally, sales associates can be requested to give some thought to their goals for the coming twelve months prior to the goal setting meeting with the broker.

When the broker meets with each sales associate to set goals, the discussion can be structured in the following way:

Exhibit 18
Sample Goal Setting Form

Goals for 19_____ for (Name)_____

Analyze your ability, experience, knowledge and motivation.
Study your past performance. Based on this analysis decide on
goals for the coming year.

1. *Listings:* I plan to obtain _____ listings per month =

   _____ listings per year.
   To achieve this goal, I plan to use the following listing sources:

   1. _____   4. _____

   2. _____   5. _____

   3. _____   6. _____

2. *Sales:* I plan to make _____ sales per month = _____ sales per
   year.
   To achieve this goal, I plan to use the following prospect sources.

   1. _____   4. _____

   2. _____   5. _____

   3. _____   6. _____

3. *My income goal* for this year is $_____ .

4. *Work:* I plan to work _____ hours per week = _____ hours
   this year.

5. *Personal Development:* To further my personal development and

   growth I plan to _____

   by (date) _____ .

---

*Step 1. Have the sales associate present his tentative goals for
the coming year.*

One of the most effective ways of opening the goal setting discussion is for the broker to invite the sales associate to share his
thinking on possible goals for the coming year. In this manner the

broker can begin to get an understanding of the sales associate's thinking.

Step 2. The broker should discuss each goal with the sales associate.
Essentially, the broker will interview the sales associate about his goals. Again the basic listening skills find application. If the broker feels the goal is too ambitious or too limited he should share this opinion with the sales associate. The principal thrust of the discussion should be directed toward trying to understand the sales associate's reasoning in setting the goals.

Goal setting discussions structure the kind of discourse which can provide a unique opportunity for learning about the motivations of the sales associate. In other words, *the reasoning behind the goals is as important as the goals themselves.*

Step 3. Agree on the goal.
Hopefully, the outcome of the discussion will be agreement between broker and sales associate on each goal. To the extent the sales associate agrees with the goal, his motivation to achieve it will be high. On the other hand, the broker wants the goals to be reasonably difficult and to reflect his plans for the business.

Step 4. Agree on how the sales person is going to try to meet the goal.
Often this will be discussed while agreeing on the goal. In any event, the broker and sales associate should discuss and agree on the strategies the person is going to pursue to meet each goal.

Step 5. Agree on a time frame for a follow-up discussion.
Once goals and strategies for achieving them are agreed on, the broker should indicate approximately when he is planning to follow up with the sales associate to discuss progress toward the goals. This follow-up should happen in two to three months from the time of the goal setting discussion.

In other words, goal setting is a planning process. The broker and sales associate are planning the sales associate's business results and personal development activities for the coming twelve months. This planning is an important part of the appraisal process. People should be appraised against their goals. To the extent goals are not clearly set, appraisals become a nebulous and unnecessarily haphazard business.

Frequent Progress Reviews

Once goals are set the broker is in a position to hold frequent interim reviews. These reviews are not appraisals but progress

Exhibit 19
Structuring the Goal Setting Discussion

Sales associate prepares goals in preparation for discussion.

a. Have the sales associate present his goals.
b. Discuss each goal with the sales associate.
c. Agree on the goal.
d. Agree on how the person is going to try to meet the goal.
e. Agree on a time frame for a follow-up discussion.

reports and problem solving sessions. Nevertheless they are a critical part of the appraisal process. As the broker conducts these interim reviews he has an opportunity to:

- Help the sales associate to improve his performance.
- Analyze the sales associate's strengths and weaknesses which provide a sound basis for appraising performance.

Exhibit 20 illustrates the role of the interim review in the appraisal process using the outline of a football field. At one end of the field, goals are set. As we march down the field a series of interim reviews are conducted. As indicated by the arrows alongside the field, the broker uses these reviews to help the sales associate adjust his strategy to improve his performance. However, as these adjustments are tried, the broker gradually learns more about the sales associate's strengths and weaknesses. By the end of the field, the broker will have a considerable experience base on which to appraise the sales associate.

This process is similar to what a good coach does during a football game. As his team marches downfield, he continually makes adjustments in strategy, such as changing blocking assignments and pass patterns, to help his players succeed with the game plan. Gradually, however, he also arrives at certain conclusions about the capabilities of his personnel. As his adjustments succeed or fail he learns about the potential and developmental needs of his players. A good manager goes through a similar process as his people try to succeed with the yearly game plan embodied in their goals.

Interim reviews do not, of course, take the place of the continuing discussion about performance which characterizes virtually any good sales office. What they do is structure a situation in which performance to date on all of the goals is discussed in a single

Exhibit 20
Appraisal System Overview

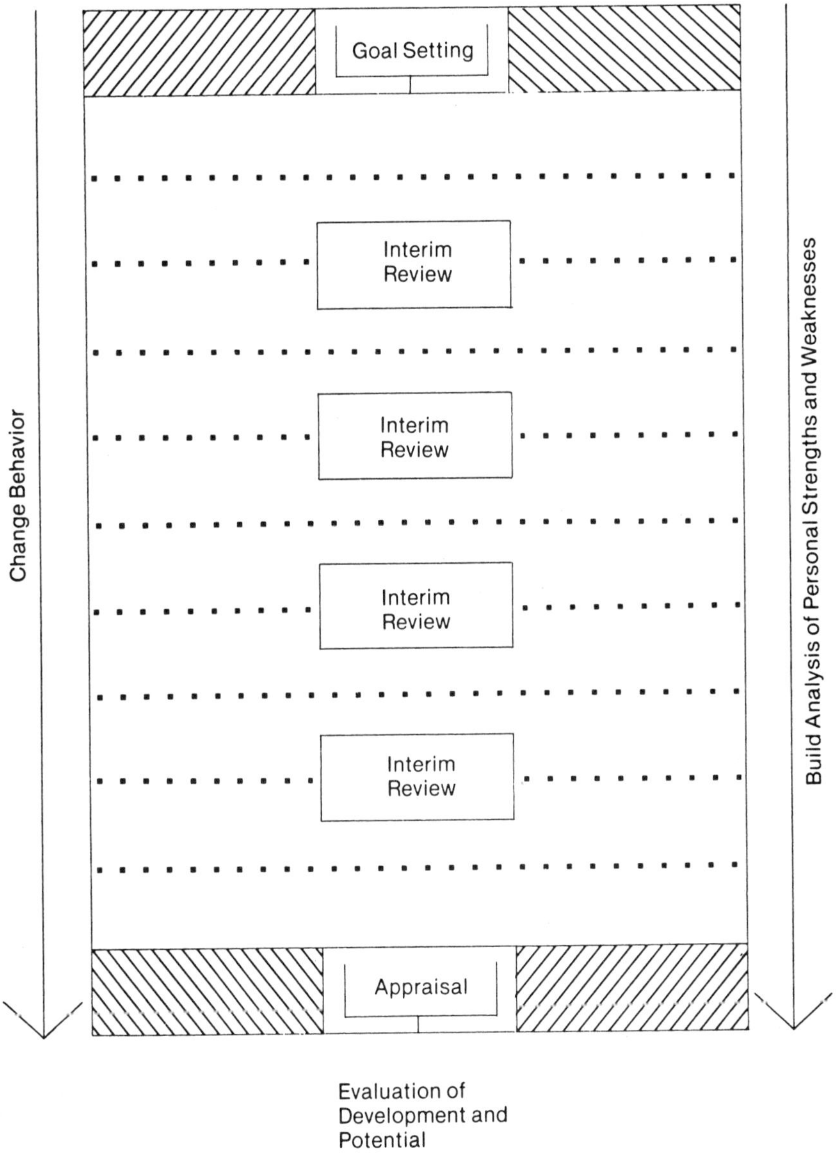

Goal Setting

Interim Review

Interim Review

Interim Review

Interim Review

Appraisal

Change Behavior

Build Analysis of Personal Strengths and Weaknesses

Evaluation of
Development and
Potential

setting, providing both parties with an opportunity to quietly assess what has been happening. Such structured reviews are especially important for brokers who feel that they do not otherwise do as thorough a job as they should in discussing performance problems with their people.

Research indicates that effective interim reviews are the key to the success of a goal-based appraisal system. When managers hold such reviews on a regular basis their people are much more likely to achieve their goals. Further, both the manager and the sales associate are more likely to find the goal setting process helpful for managing performance when frequent reviews are held. In light of this research, it makes sense for a broker who believes strongly in the value of goal setting to follow through with interim reviews.

How to Conduct a Progress Review

It naturally follows that the reviews have to be well managed if maximum benefits are to be realized. In conducting the interim review, the broker once again should posture the discussion so that the basic flow of information is from the sales associate to the broker. This can be accomplished by the broker saying something like:

"As we've discussed before, from time to time I want to review the progress you have made toward your goals in order to be sure we take advantage of every opportunity to help you succeed. I think putting aside a little time just to focus on your goals is the best way to accomplish this. Let's begin with you telling me where you stand on each of your goals."

The sales associate can now tell the broker how much progress he has made on each goal. Every goal should be discussed separately, regardless of whether the sales associate is on target or behind in his progress. Unfortunately, some brokers tend to skip over the goals which are being met, and spend time only on the ones which progress has been lacking. As one broker put it, "I spend time on the areas which need improvement. The goals they are accomplishing speak for themselves." This is unfortunate because it overlooks opportunities for enhancing communication between the broker and sales associate.

When a sales associate is making good progress toward a goal, probing the reasons for this success accomplishes three things:

First, the broker provides recognition of the sales associate's accomplishments. Even though the broker already knows about the sales associate's success to date, discussing it is important. As one successful broker remarked, "They like to know I know exactly how hard they have worked."

Second, discussing *how* the person has been achieving his goals gives the broker the opportunity to stress how important these activities are. In so doing, the broker provides guidance to the sales associate. (Of course, there is the chance that the broker will learn that the sales associate has been using certain approaches which the broker feels are inappropriate. For example, one sales associate was making promises to buyers which could get the firm into legal conflicts. The broker took immediate corrective action.)

Third, exploring why a sales associate has been successful provides important insights for the broker's appraisal. Often the same personal characteristics which create problems in one area, account for success in another. In this fashion, the broker gets a more complete picture of the sales associate's abilities.

Thus, when the sales associate indicates he is right on schedule with a goal, the broker wants to invite the sales associate to discuss his progress. For example:

Sales Associate:	Well, let's begin with my sales goal. As you know, I set a goal of 30 sales for the year. For the past three months I have sold three houses each month, which puts me well ahead of schedule for this time of the year. In fact, I was expecting to do an average of only two a month this quarter.
Broker:	Yes, I am aware of that. Your performance to date this year has been excellent. What do you think explains it?
Sales Associate:	Well ... in thinking about the market I noticed ...

Above we see how a self–appraisal question, which we learned about in Chapter 5, finds application in this situation. In fact all of the interviewing skills do. That's because an interim review is really another form of interviewing. In selection interviewing we are attempting to assess what accounts for a candidate's success in the past in order to predict his likely performance in real estate. During the interim review we are attempting to assess what accounts for an associate's current performance so that we can increase future effectiveness. There is an analogy between the two situations. In other words, *subject the sales associate's current performance to the same careful analysis as prior experiences were subjected to during the selection process.*

Goals in which progress has been less than expected must, of course, also be explored in depth. Here the broker is in a problem solving mode, using the approaches learned in Chapter 4, but instead of approaching the associate about a particular problem, he is responding to the sales associate's lack of progress toward the goal.

Exhibit 21 illustrates the two possible communication flows which can typify the problem solving process for a lagging goal. Once the sales associate indicates he is behind on a goal, the broker begins to ask self–appraisal questions to explore the problem. At this point one of two things will occur.

Exhibit 21
Two Possible Problem-solving Flows

Sales Associate states he is behind on a goal.
Broker asks: *What Seems to be the Problem?*

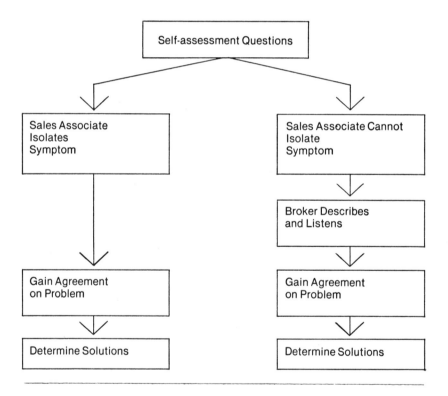

One is that in response to the questions, the sales associate will begin to isolate some of the symptoms and begin the process of identifying the real problem. This flow is illustrated on the left of Exhibit 21.

The other is that the sales associate will have difficulty isolating the symptoms which are preventing progress. Then the broker will have to try to help the problem solving process along by adding more of his own input. This is done in a descriptive fashion. The broker will describe any situations he has observed which may have bearing on the problem. At this point the broker is in the basic problem solving sequence recommended in Chapter 4. The flow on the right of Exhibit 21 illustrates this sequence.

Consider the following example of this problem solving sequence:

Sales Associate:	Well, as you probably realize, I am not as far along as we planned in meeting my sales objectives. In fact, I am three transactions behind. This, of course, puts me behind on my income goals as well.
Broker:	What seems to be the problem?
Sales Associate:	I don't know really. I just seem to be unlucky in that I have gotten a lot of prospects who aren't serious about buying. I know I have been putting in a lot of effort.
Broker:	I know you have been working hard. What do you mean about the prospects?
Sales Associate:	Well, they seem interested in looking. But they hedge when it comes to making an offer.
Broker:	You feel they aren't really ready to buy.
Sales Associate:	It seems that way.
Broker:	Well, I've noticed something which might help us here. While you show a house really well, you tend to pull back when the prospect is making the buying decision. Remember, when the couple from Phoenix were looking at the Scottsdale property? You said nothing while they discussed the advantages of buying. Later they bought a similar value in town from Johnson Associates.
Sales Associate:	Well, I feel people resent a pushy salesperson. People will buy when they are ready.

Broker:	I noticed the same thing with the prospect from out of town who was in the office yesterday. While they compared properties, instead of closing you largely left them alone.
Sales Associate:	Well, again I didn't want to be pushy.
Broker:	What makes you think closing is bad?
Sales Associate:	Well ... I am uncomfortable. It is just my nature not to force people into a decision.
Broker:	Let's see if you can't do something about it ...

As we can see, the broker is identifying a personality-related performance problem. Once he and the sales associate agree on the problem they can explore specific types of skills which would help the sales associate overcome her problem. Specifically, in the case on which this dialogue is based, he taught her how to compare the advantages of alternative buys in a way that leads into a close. They practiced the technique through role play.

In this instance, the solution worked because of the sales associate's overwhelming motivation to succeed. Gradually she improved her skills in this area, although she recognizes that her natural inclinations are to back off. Lacking this strong motivation to succeed, the review process would have probably led to the conclusion that she was not really well suited for the sales role.

Notice how during the above exchange the broker was descriptive in his input, and how he used questions effectively to facilitate the communication process. This is one more illustration of the general application of these skills.

This process of examining progress can be repeated for each goal.

If the broker has several interim review meetings over the course of the year with each associate, two things will gradually be accomplished. First, he will systematically assist his people in meeting their goals. Second, a sound appraisal of each person's current level of development will emerge.

The Summary Appraisal

At the end of the time period for which the goals were set (usually twelve months) the broker is ready to provide his appraisal of each person's performance. This is a feedback session during which the broker shares his perceptions of the person's performance.

If the interim review sessions have been held, there should be few surprises. First, the sales associate will have either met his goals or not met them. Second, many of the reasons why will have been explored throughout the course of the year.

Thus, the twelve month appraisal is the time for the broker to pull together a summary portrait of the sales associate's performance. Most importantly, the broker should present his opinions on what the implications are for next year's goals.

For example, the year's experience will suggest what level of performance is realistic for the coming year. It might also suggest certain personal development goals, such as improving sales techniques.

Basically, the broker should take a balance sheet approach to the appraisal, covering the sales associate's strong points and those areas which are in need of development. In this discussion the broker takes the lead.

He can begin with a comment like "Over the course of the year we have discussed your progress toward your goals. Now that we know how you finally did, I would like to share with you my impressions. I would like to build on this experience for next year. Let me first share with you what clearly stands out as your strengths. Then we can focus on areas for improvement. First, one thing which really impressed me was. . ."

The broker should go on to share his appraisal, relating his comments to the salesperson's original goals. One of the questions frequently asked is whether the person's strengths or weaknesses should be presented first. While communication research does not provide a clearcut answer to this question, experience indicates that whichever is presented first tends to set the tone for the discussion. Therefore, if the person's performance has been generally good, the positives should be discussed first. Then the broker can move on to areas needing improvement, ending with a discussion of possible personal development steps. However, if the individual's performance has been poor to the point of demanding improvement if the association is to be continued, then the issue should be discussed first to avoid any confusion or doubt about the seriousness of the situation. Then the broker can end by noting whatever strengths exist.

Exhibit 22 provides some general guidelines for the appraisal discussion.

Appraisal Is an Integrated Management System

When the sales associate leaves the appraisal he should be encouraged to share any observations or comments which later come

Exhibit 22
Structuring the Appraisal Meeting

■ Grows out of the interim review discussions. The broker takes the lead, evaluating the staff person based on goal achievement and the review discussions.

■ Present strengths to provide positive feedback
provides recognition of accomplishments
communictes direction for the future

■ Present weaknesses and development needs
provides input for future development

■ When discussing strengths and weaknesses
point out how each led to goals being met or missed related to the obstacles encountered elicit discussion

■ Discuss development steps and possible implications for next year's goals.

to mind. Most importantly, he should use the appraisal discussion to develop his goals for the coming year.

Taken together, the three elements of the appraisal process—goal setting, interim reviews, and the twelve month appraisal—represent an integrated performance planning and control system. This system is not intended to replace the other communication which occurs in the sales office. Rather, it is a formal process which insures that total performance is systematically emphasized over the course of the year.

Of course, the process described above requires an investment of time on the part of the broker. For this reason it is imperative that goals be written only for those areas which are critical to the sales associate's performance and development. By keeping the number of goals to a minimum, the time investment in each meeting becomes more reasonable. Further, it insures that each discussion will relate to the needs of the office. Thus, the process is not one more thing the broker is supposed to do. The appraisal process becomes integrated into the management operation.

From the sales associate's side, it eliminates what one sales manager described as "the annual keep your job contest" which typifies some growing firms. The sales associate receives continuing support in his effort to achieve his sales goals. This is the bottom line in management communication.

Chapter 8
Awkward Communication Problems

Every broker faces awkward communication problems. They can be challenging, irritating, time-consuming and, if not properly resolved, a drain on the business. Let's consider six such problems which have been identified by prominent brokers.

Opinions differ as to how a broker should handle these situations. In part, the solution must reflect the personality of the firm. However, experience teaches us that there are guidelines which characterize the effective resolution of certain problems.

Non-Voluntary Termination

Almost no one looks forward to firing another person. Terminating a sales associate is one of the most difficult managerial tasks which confronts a broker. Yet it has to be done. Letting ineffective sales people "hang on" is a major weakness in management. Not only are they a drain on the firm's resources, but they can be a drag on the morale of the other salespeople, eventually destroying the esprit de corps. There are at least four reasons for terminating a sales associate.

Lack of Production The most obvious reason for terminating someone is when his production is below the minimal standards set by the broker. And every broker should have such standards. Letting someone hang around in the hope that he will make a sale or two is an inefficient way of running an office. Every successful firm striving for a secure piece of the market needs a relatively stable cadre of top performers. Equally important is a healthy turnover of poor performers. Turnover here brings fresh blood into the firm and can generate an atmosphere of "only the best can make it here."

Abrasive Personalities A less obvious reason for termination is an abrasive personality. Here, of course, we are talking about the extreme case where a sales associate's ego leads him to behave in ways which interfere with the work of others. The key is *behavior.* When specific behaviors are obviously preventing others from performing well (such as the sales associate trying to show up a colleague in front of a buyer or interjecting himself into the affairs of others) and repeated reprimands produce no change, termination must be considered. Such individuals are usually highly destructive to office morale.

Ethical Problems Violation of license laws or other sales practices which violate firm policy, such as commission cutting, should be grounds for termination. Remember, such practices reflect on the image of the firm and everyone associated with it. Failure to deal with such problems constitutes tacit approval of the practices involved.

Violation of Firm's Policy and Procedures Failure to meet floor time, follow qualifying procedures or complete required paperwork are all examples of possible violation of firm rules. When after repeated reprimands a sales associate fails to conform to the rules, the broker must either back up the rule with termination or terminate the rule. Before opting to back off from the rule the broker should remember that other salespeople will "test" him on other rules as well. At some point the broker will have to start enforcing the rules or lose control of his firm. Therefore, failure to enforce a rule because of a desire to avoid conflict only postpones the inevitable.

Handling Terminations

Termination will generally be preceded by a series of discussions. A broker who suddenly springs termination on a sales associate hasn't been doing his job as a manager. Neither is the broker who just waits, hoping the sales associate will leave.

A situation which might lead to termination should be immediately addressed in the form of constructive criticism.[1] If attempts at constructive criticism and problem solving fail, the broker must readdress the situation, stating flatly that efforts toward resolving the problem have proved ineffective and if the situation does not correct itself shortly, the broker feels it will be in the best interest of both parties to terminate the relationship. The broker should clearly specify to the sales associate what he means by *shortly*.

In this fashion, the stage is set for terminating the sales associate while minimizing the possibility the broker is cutting off someone who could be salvaged for the firm. And, depending on the circumstances, the entire process does not require a drawn out period of time. When evidence of a problem emerges, the broker should initiate a problem solving discussion as soon as possible. Once it becomes clear that the problem is not being resolved, the remainder of the process can move along very quickly.

Of course, many salespeople will terminate themselves once they sense they are not making progress. Having concrete goals and a clearly written policy and procedures manual usually facilitates the termination process. These management tools make it easy for the broker to describe problem behavior.

If a termination interview proves necessary, the broker should come straight to the point. Beating around the bush makes the broker appear indecisive and the situation becomes more difficult to handle. The broker should begin the conversation with something like, "Bob, I am really very sorry, but I am going to have to let you go. We've talked about this issue before and . . ." Once he has informed the sales associate of his decision, the broker should not entertain any reasons for retaining the individual. Some salespeople will try to "sell" the broker on giving them one more shot. At this point, however, last ditch efforts virtually always fail. The broker should listen but make it clear the decision is not reversible.

Above all else, the broker should avoid agreeing to any special conditions as part of the termination process. Because we are often uncomfortable when letting someone go, we may be susceptible to requests which we normally would turn down. Thus, it is best to make no promises during the interview itself. It is also best for the sales associate to collect his things and leave the office as soon as possible once the interview is over.

Despite the straightforwardness of the termination process, the decision to terminate should not be mechanical. In every case the broker is weighing the seriousness of the problem against the sales associate's potential for development. The case of Ann and Susan illustrates this point.

Ann and Susan joined the firm at the same time. Both were in their late thirties. At the end of the first year the two women had identical production records which were only half what the broker expected from a new person.

Ann was gregarious and had a pleasant personality. Her husband was head of a large business. It seemed like everyone in town knew her.

However, Ann's husband was strongly opposed to her real estate activity and gave her no support at home. Further, Ann's behavior seemed to suggest that she questioned the value of sales work. Lacking social ease when closing, Ann would show houses, not sell them.

Susan was an extremely hard working individual. Although she did not have Ann's extensive community contacts, she was effective at meeting people. Additionally, she was always positive about her career goals. Having had money in a previous marriage, Susan seemed sure of the life style she wanted to maintain. She also had strong support from her second husband.

Although like Ann's, Susan's first year was unsuccessful, the broker felt he could see several of the right motivational signs of success. She had problems, but was working hard on them. The broker terminated Ann and retained Susan.

During Susan's second year with the firm her sales skills matured. Today she is one that firm's best salespeople.

Ann joined another firm, failed there and is now out of real estate.

Judgment, based on close communication with the people involved, is always part of the termination decision.

Voluntary Termination

Another kind of termination problem is the successful sales associate who decides to join another firm or to leave to establish one of his own.

When a highly valued sales associate announces he is joining another firm, the first question the broker usually asks is, "How firm is the decision to leave?" To be frank, however, the decision to leave is usually final. In fact, if the broker has been taken by surprise he has probably been missing some pretty strong signals from the sales associate during the previous couple of months.

At this point, the broker needs to assess what, if anything, might have been done to avert this situation. Personnel professionals know it is difficult to get a true picture of the departing person's feelings during an interview. Most agree, however, that it is worth a try. Sometimes simply stating, "Look, I respect your decision. Speaking as friends, what things were involved in your decision to leave?" As with many of the communication situations described in this book, the sales associate's first response seldom tells the whole story. Probing and careful listening are usually required if the broker is going to get any sense of the other person's real feelings.

Assessing the situation objectively will be difficult. Many sentiments are likely to cloud the broker's perception: concern over losing a good producer, defensiveness over the implicit suggestion that the grass is greener elsewhere, worry over the impact on other members of the firm, etc. Thus, it is probably wise to reassess the situation again after the person has left.

It makes little sense to communicate hostility or ill feelings toward the sales associate. As a practical matter it is best to suggest that the two of you will still be friends, but competitors, and likely cooperators in the future.

Much of the above is true of the top sales associate who decides to open his own firm. This is a common problem for the REALTOR®. Since it is a predictable occurrence, anticipating preventive measures is the best strategy.

Seldom does a top producer really want to be a manager-broker. Usually the decision to start one's own firm is rooted in a strong need for recognition. Thus, providing recognition for the top producers on a regular basis through awards, newspaper coverage, and inviting these associates to make presentations at sales meetings is an important part of maintaining job satisfaction. And involve top producers in some management decisions to which they can make a real contribution.

Even more important is helping the sales associate understand what he really enjoys about real estate and where his true strengths lie. The formal appraisal process discussed in Chapter 7 can be a good vehicle for accomplishing this self–insight. As the broker reviews the sales associate's performance over the past year and presents his opinions of the person's abilities, the appraisal can lead to the self–realization that selling is where his true interests and strengths lie. Many a top salesperson has resisted the tendency to set up his own firm because he has come to understand his strengths and weaknesses.

Complementary to the strategy of encouraging realistic personal assessment is making sure the top performer has sound knowledge of the problems and costs of running and owning a firm. Once a salesperson has announced his intention to set up his own shop, it is not likely the broker can change his mind. An effective response is for the broker to offer some basic advice as to things the salesperson should take care of immediately in establishing his office (thus subtly telling the salesperson what he is getting into).

Wish the person well. If he has been a truly valuable sales associate, tell him that *should he decide he prefers straight sales,* he is welcome back. Avoid using language like *"if things don't work out"* since it clearly suggests returning would be a sign of failure rather than personal preference.

Managing the Superstar

John, a sales associate in a midwestern company, delivered an ultimatum to his broker; "A more favorable commission split or I leave."

Fred, a salesperson in an eastern firm, wanted an equity deal.

Janette, a member of a New England firm, wanted special consideration with a property she wanted to purchase.

Nancy, in the southwest, complains regularly about the lack of secretarial support.

Louise, discontent over not being named sales manager, is a continual problem, stirring up trouble with the other sales associates.

These people share one very important thing in common. Each is his firm's biggest producer.

Managing the superstar can become a love/hate relationship for a broker. Their production is great, but so are the problems which go along with it.

Of course, not all superstars are problems. But, for those that are, effective management alleviates many problem situations.

One west coast broker with a large firm has seen many of his superstars move through career stages. His description is supported by the experiences of other brokers. It also suggests opportunities for effective management of these sales associates.

Stage One—The Ego Stage Ego is always an important motivator for the superstar. It is especially dominant early in a selling career.

Consider the situation. Suddenly the superstar's career is taking off. His success has significantly surpassed that of most of his peers. He's a big winner.

During this period recognition of his special status is important. The superstar accumulates the status symbols which provide this recognition. His life style improves dramatically.

During this stage the star is looking to the broker for recognition as well. Prizes and awards are especially important; so is recognition at sales meetings. The star expects the broker to recognize him in dealings with the local community.

Stage Two—Maturity Over time, the superstar grows comfortable with his status. He is sustaining a relatively high life style. The status symbols have been acquired.

Most importantly, he understands the business skills which have made him a success. He keeps his floor time, he qualifies prospects and concentrates his efforts on the most promising and he is organized. Often he will include other sales associates in some of his deals, utilizing his time more effectively and integrating himself into the needs of his colleagues.

At this point in the superstar's career, ego needs are important, but they are being satisfied. Should the recognition stop, our superstar would be upset. But as long as the broker continues to provide recognition his needs are satisfied. His ego is a foundation of his success, not a continual thirst.

It is during this stage that the broker has the opportunity to lay the groundwork for managing these sales associates during the next phase of their careers. Sound appraisals, which help the star understand his true strengths should be part of the broker's communication strategy. Maturity brings with it a willingness to analyze success. For a brief period, the broker has an opportunity to emphasize the value of his being part of the firm—the technical assistance in closing commercial deals, the financial assistance which helps put a deal together, the prestige of advertising and the firm's name, and freedom from administrative details.

Stage Three—The Identity Crisis It may begin gradually, but the signs are unmistakable. The star begins to test the broker. He wants a better commission split, or special consideration on a property he plans to purchase, or a piece of the action.

Almost inevitably the superstar begins to think about being in business for himself. Is he better off as a salesperson or should he be a broker with his name on the door? The personal recognition of owning a business has a strong attraction. He starts to test the broker, looking for special privileges, while he decides what to do.

The outcome of this stage is partly determined by how the broker has managed the star. If the broker has "wheeled and dealed" against the star, the star is more likely to "wheel and deal" back. If the firm has a strong professional image in the community, the star will probably be aware of the formidable competition he'll face on his own.

Regardless, experience argues strongly in favor of the following guidelines for dealing with the star in this stage:

Never renegotiate business arrangements in the face of an ultimatum.

Don't give special consideration to the superstar unless such consideration will be available to all top performers as a matter of policy.

Do address signs of discontent immediately. They will almost always get worse and begin to affect the whole staff.

Do continue to provide recognition to the star.

Do continue to describe the advantages of being associated with the firm.

Accept the fact that as important as the star's production is to the sales volume of the firm, over the long haul the office will be more productive in the absence of a destructive superstar.

Realistically, the star will sometimes opt to stay; other times he will leave. Once his decision is made, the star reverts back to the maturity stage, at least for the time being. In the future, other identity crises may arise as the star once again assesses his situation.

Resentment Toward the New Offices

For nine years Marie Johnson owned a firm with eight to ten sales people. Then, the local market began to expand and Marie expanded with it. As the firm grew in size, Marie began to extend the geographic scope of her operations. She opened a couple of branch offices.

Suddenly, Marie had twenty-five to twenty-nine people in three offices. With this growth came a whole new set of problems. For example:

Many of the old timers complained about the loss of family feeling in the firm. More than one sales associate commented that he felt left out. One said, "We used to be like a close-knit family. Now it's as though the in-laws have moved in."

Conflicts between offices emerged as sales associates from one office resented those from other offices coming into their territory.

Sales associates in the original office, which was located in a very affluent area, looked upon their colleagues in the other branches in a condescending fashion. This sentiment was especially directed toward one of the branches which serviced a significantly less affluent area.

Marie's problems are representative of those faced by growing firms: new offices are viewed as the competition rather than as extensions of the same team.

Such conflicts are largely unavoidable. When the broker decides to add branches, he is accepting the responsibility for having to manage them.[2] Some do a better job of managing these conflicts than others.

Managing Interbranch Conflict

The types of conflicts described above are expressions of sentiment. In this case the sentiments are rooted in resistance to change. Part of a managerial strategy for dealing with the conflicts generated by this sentiment is to attack it at its source by reducing the sales associates' resistance to change. In part this can be accomplished by:

- Preselling the new branches to staff *before* they are established. Emphasize how the expansion can strengthen the firm's reputation, promising opportunities for all firm members who are motivated to take advantage of them. The broker should be frank about how he hopes constructive competition will exist between branches, just as a strong sales office has a competitive atmosphere. However, this competition will not be permitted to become destructive. It will be to everyone's benefit to cooperate with one another within the framework of the firm's policy and procedures manual.
- Preselling has an added advantage of forewarning the broker of the kinds of specific reactions with which he will have to deal.
- Involving sales associates in the planning for the new offices. *People tend to support what they helped create.* Translated into communication this means it is to the broker's advantage to solicit the opinions of his salespeople on issues affecting the new offices and listen carefully to them.

Discussion of preliminary plans *before* they have been finalized at sales meetings can facilitate the communication process. This is especially true if various sales associates hold conflicting opinions about the proposed expansion. Behavorial science clearly teaches us that group discussion helps mitigate such conflicting viewpoints.[3] As they hear their peers express opposing viewpoints, the tendency is for most sales associates to understand the various arguments more clearly. Further, as they express their own viewpoints, resistance tends to lessen.

Throughout the process of soliciting the opinions of his sales associates, it is important that the broker make it clear that he is not asking them to decide whether or not to expand (unless, of course, he really is asking them to help him make a decision). Rather, the broker should be explicit that he is seeking their input so he has the advantage of having their thoughts as he makes decisions regarding the new branches. If the sales associates aren't clear as to the exact nature of their participation, they can feel they are being manipulated.

Once the new branch has opened, those sales associates who harbor doubts about the effect the new branch will have on their own situation are likely to focus on the differences between the offices. Differences are often perceived as being "wrong" or "inferior". The broker can counter this trend somewhat by creating situations which help establish similarities and familiarities between the offices. For example:

- Training should be standardized for all offices.
- Have all new sales associates' orientation include a visit to each of the branches to spend time with an experienced salesperson in that office.
- All offices should operate under the same policies and procedures.
- Schedule periodic joint sales meetings.
- Sponsor periodic social or recognition events which bring together members of the different offices.
- Give sales managers the job of transmitting the advantages of growth to their people.

Practices such as these will not eliminate conflicts between offices. But they will create a climate in which it is easier for the broker to manage the conflict.

When a sales associate voices dissatisfaction about other branch offices, his concern should be addressed directly and within the framework of the conflict management model previously learned.

Opening new offices is a commitment to growth. Every broker must decide what his firm is going to be: a small organization built around a key group of sales people, or a large, growing organization. A commitment to growth means sacrificing the "family" atmosphere. Further, a growing firm must continue growing to truly achieve the advantages of size. The smart broker won't have any uncertainty on this point.

Getting the "Old Hands" to Accept New Associates

Unfortunately, experienced salespeople sometimes resist the new salesperson. New people make mistakes and the established associate may react with comments such as, "They are hurting our professional image." The beginner senses this attitude. As one new sales associate put it, "It's the pits. Surrounded by success, I feel like an idiot."

There is no substitute for an extensive training and orientation program to minimize the impact of this problem. A good training program gives new people confidence while experienced sales associates can see the beginners progress. Of course, the broker can remind the veterans how it was when they were starting out.

When an experienced sales associate indicates concern over new salespeople, his real worry is usually more personal than the mistakes a beginner makes. What he really wants to discuss is his feeling that growth means a smaller piece of the pie for him.

There are two points the broker needs to make with this sales associate.

"First, all salespeople, whether old or new, are only going to succeed if they perform. The salesperson who keeps his floor time, qualifies his prospects, and organizes his time well does well regardless of who joins the firm."

"Second, if the firm is comprised only of people who perform in this fashion, the pie will grow as a result of the new people. And, I intend to retain only people who perform."

Administrative Support People

As has been suggested throughout this book, clerical support people are important to maintaining a smoothly functioning sales office. The astute broker is as concerned with his administrative, salaried staff as he is with his salespeople.

The receptionist-secretary, for example, often presents the firm's first impression to prospective clients. If she is skillful at putting people at ease, the buyer or seller immediately feels that perhaps this is a good place to do business. The buyer who is new in town begins to sense an initial comfortableness in strange surroundings.

Leaving the selection and training of administrative staff to happenstance lays the groundwork for gaping holes in a firm's ability to function. All of the managerial communication models presented in this book are applicable to salaried staff.

Care must be taken to integrate office support people into the sales organization. Periodic participation in sales meetings when items relating to the firm's administration are on the agenda is one way to accomplish this. Members of the administrative staff can lead problem-solving discussions on topics that affect the sales staff.

For example, perhaps certain months traditionally have a high number of closings, which puts unusual job pressures on the closing department. As work gets backed up, complaints increase from salespeople who want the paperwork "immediately" and staff tensions increase. The problem can be discussed at a sales meeting shortly before the anticipated busy period. Sales associates can be instructed to identify as far in advance as possible the critical instances where the closing date can make or break the deal. The need for salespeople to be knowledgable about the volume of work in the closing department can be stressed.

Another firm changed its procedures for paying commissions in order to comply with a new state law. Previously, commissions were paid by the closing department on the day of closing, out of trust funds. Under the new procedure, commissions would be paid once a week by bookkeeping from general funds. This meant a possible ten-day wait, depending on the day of closing.

Again, conflicts between salaried and salespeople were generated. Salespeople pressured closing officers on last-minute closings to get the work finished in time to collect their commissions that week. Further, salespeople complained to bookkeepers about having to wait for their money.

This problem is another example where including administrative and salespeople in team-oriented sales meetings can help resolve conflict through problem solving. At a series of such meetings, it was agreed by both bookkeeping and sales that paying commissions twice a week was a compromise solution. By adopting certain procedures, bookkeeping could issue the checks and the salespeople were satisfied. This is a good illustration of how addressing conflict in a manner which encourages examination of all points of view leads to acceptable alternatives.

It was further agreed that the closing department had a strict deadline for accepting deals for the current commission period and no exceptions would be permitted. Since the waiting period for commissions had been cut in half, the sales staff were more tolerant of the needs of the closing department.

The above cases illustrate an important point: the sales "team" must include the entire office, not just sales associates.

Salaried people should be included in social events sponsored by the firm. As the firm grows, and new branches are opened, a company newsletter can provide everyone with a sense of identity with the company.

Communication is a process of understanding. The broker has communicated only when a staff member has understood his message. To the extent the broker perceives the needs of his people, he is in a better position to communicate with them. Industrial consultants agree that one of the most difficult tasks which confronts any management team is getting people to talk effectively *with* one another. This does not happen automatically. It requires skillful managerial practices. But the benefits in terms of production and cost avoidance are substantial.

Footnotes for Chapter 8

1. See Chapter 4.

2. See Chapter 3.

3. Victor Vroom and Philip Yetton, *Leadership and Decision Making* (Pittsburgh: University of Pittsburgh Press, 1973).

Selected Bibliography

Brennan, John, *The Conscious Communicator* (Reading, Mass: Addison-Wesley, 1974)

The Competitive Edge in Selling Real Estate (Chicago: REALTORS NATIONAL MARKETING INSTITUTE®, 1979).

Drake, John D., *Interviewing for Managers* (New York: AMACOM, 1972).

Levy, Seymour, *Improving Performance Through Performance Review* (New Rochelle: M. M. Bruce, 1970).

Lopex, Felix M., *Personnel Interviewing* (New York: McGraw-Hill, 1965).

Moore, Robert E., *The Human Side of Successful Communication* (Englewood Cliffs: Prentice-Hall, 1961).

Morris, John C., *Make Yourself Clear* (New York: McGraw-Hill, 1972).

Nierenberg, Gerard I., *The Art of Negotiating* (New York: Hawthorne Books, 1976).

Nierenberg, Jesse S., *Getting Through to People* (Englewood Cliffs: Prentice-Hall, 1963).

Prince, George M., *The Practice of Creativity* (New York: Harper & Row, 1970).

Real Estate Office Management: People, Functions, Systems (Chicago: REALTORS NATIONAL MARKETING INSTITUTE®, 1975).

Real Estate Sales Handbook, 8th Edition (Chicago: REALTORS NATIONAL MARKETING INSTITUTE®, 1979).

Real Estate Sales Meetings (Chicago: REALTORS NATIONAL MARKETING INSTITUTE®, 1976)

real estate today®: Ten Years of the Best (Chicago: REALTORS NATIONAL MARKETING INSTITUTE®, 1978).

Truell, George P., *How To Manage for More Profitable Results* (Chicago: The Dartnell Corporation, 1974).

Your Policy and Procedure Manual (Chicago: REALTORS NATIONAL MARKETING INSTITUTE®, 1974).

Index

Achievement
   and motivation, 137, 139–140
   as specific need, 97
   opportunity for, 97
Active listening, 17, 104
   See also Listening skills
Administrative support people, 3, 173–175
Adversary posture, 46, 48, 51
Agreement, obtaining, 57
Alternatives, 55–57
Applied intelligence, 100
Aptitude, 72–73, 81
Assessment, 89–122
  and the selection interview, 89
  of intelligence, 100–101
  of knowledge and experience, 100
  of motivation, 98–99
  of personality, 98–99
Attitudes, 95–96, 124
Audio-visual aids, 125
Autocratic approach, 39–40
   See also Managerial grid, Managerial style

Balance sheet, 111–115
Behavioral change, 79–81
Belongingness needs, 134
Blake, Robert, 38, 40
Broad-brush questions, 20, 103–104, 110, 117–118
  defined, 104
  use of, 18, 104
   See also Questions
Bureaucratic approach, 40
   See Also Managerial grid, Managerial style

Clarity, 49, 53
Clerical support people, 3, 4
Close-ended questions, 17–20, 30–31
  defined, 18
  use of, 18–19
  v. open-ended, 30–31
  See also Questions
Coaching, 20, 126–133, 141–148
  as follow-up, 129
  feedback in, 128
  helper role in, 126, 130–133
  instructing role in, 126
  with concrete examples, 127
  using reflection, 128
  with step-by-step explanations, 127
  telling role in, 126
Communication problems, 163–175
  with abrasive personalities, 164
  with accepting new associates, 173
  with administrative support people,
    173–175
  with ethical problems, 164
  with handling terminations, 165
  with lack of production, 164
  with managing the superstar,
    168–170
  with non-voluntary terminations,
    163–166
  with resentment toward new offices,
    170–173
  with violations of policy and
    procedure, 164
  with voluntary terminations,
    166–168
Comparisons, in criticism, 84
  See also Criticism
Competition, 137
Compromise, 40
Conceptual skill, 7
Concern for people, 38–41
  See also Managerial grid,
    Managerial style
Concern for production, 38–41
  See also Managerial grid,
    Managerial style
Conflict, 37–66
  addressing, 37, 46
  adversary posture of, 46, 48, 51
  and managerial style, 38–52
  avoiding, 37, 41
  inevitability of, 37
  managing, 37, 41–58
  organizational roots of, 38
  role of perception and, 46
Conflict management model, 41–66
  avoiding argument, 52
  basic objective of, 49

criticism as a form of, 67, 68, 74
develop alternatives, 55–57
exploring differences, 51
leadership style, 48
listening skills, 52–53
need for clarity, 49, 53
obtaining agreement, 57
procrastination, 44, 46
satisfying the needs of others, 40
sharpening the differences, 54–56
Consultative approach, 40–47
  and effectiveness of organization, 40
  and effectiveness for real estate
    market, 41
Controls, 149
Cooperation, 11
Core communication skills, 16, 17–30,
    44
  as building blocks of managerial
    effectiveness, 29
  defined, 16
Country club manager, 40
  See also Managerial grid,
    Managerial style
Credibility, 42
Criticism, 26–28, 46, 49–50, 67–85
  descriptive v. evaluative, 26, 28,
    35–36, 50, 68
  guidelines for, 83–84
  intent of, 68
  of performance, 53, 68
  requires problem solving, 68
  See also Problem solving

Descriptive statements, 27–29, 35–36,
    68
  and performance criticism, 68
  based on perceptions, 28
  effective in reducing defensiveness,
    27–28, 50
  examples of, 28, 36
  guidelines for phrasing, 28–29
  v. evaluative statements, 26–28, 35,
    50, 68
  See also Criticism
Directed questions, 17, 20, 52
Discipline, 40
Drake, John, 92, 98
Drucker, Peter F., 6

Effort, 137
Emergence approach, 97–98
  See also Interviewing
Empathy, 44
End results, 127